Praise for *Badass Black Girl*

"In an era when Black girls are bombarded with negative stereotypes on traditional and social media platforms, *Badass Black Girl* offers welcome advice to Black girls to embrace their individuality and to develop positive mental and body images. Written in clear understandable prose, Fievre provides numerous examples of women such as a Toni Morrison, Michelle Obama, and Madam C. J. Walker, who exemplify Black excellence, and equips Black girls through a series of exercises and affirmations with the tools to become "Badass" women who know their worth."

—Geoffrey Philp, author of *Garvey's Ghost*

"Protecting our young Black women and femme-identifying youth is so important—M.J. Fievre lays this out with grace, care, and the most powerful love in the phenomenal *Badass Black Girl*. So often, our society tells us that we're so strong, so resilient, so able to fix everyone else's world—this book reveals the truth: Black women/femme-identifying people are just as tender, just as in need of affirmation and praise, just as worthy of an embrace from self and from those around us. This book is a celebration, an affirmation, a history text, a little bit of memoir, and an exuberant prayer for the prosperity of Black women."

—Ashley M. Jones, author of *Magic City Gospel*

"M.J. Fievre gives every girl her own set of black pearls of wisdom."

—Marie Ketsia Theodore-Pharel, author of *Beauty Walks in Nature*

"*Badass Black Girl* is the big hug you need. M.J. Fievre's newest work is a glorious love letter to the Black women who have shaped and loved us, to our griots and groundbreakers. Within these pages, Fievre celebrates Black girls in all of their power, vulnerability, and beauty and offers instructions for self-love, taking responsibility, creating art, and expressing gratitude. I wish I had this book when I was younger, and I'm happy I have it now."

—**Jennifer Maritza McCauley, author of *SCAR ON/SCAR OFF***

"You'll come away from *Badass Black Girl* feeling as if you've known the author your entire life, and it's a rare feat for any writer. M.J. Fievre is the best friend, the confidante everyone yearns for."

—**Michael Reid, "Mike, the Poet," author of *Dear Woman* and *The Boyfriend Book***

Badass
Black
Girl

Badass Black Girl

Quotes, Questions, and Affirmations for Teens

MJ Fievre

Mango Publishing

CORAL GABLES

For permission requests, please contact the publisher at:
Mango Publishing Group
2850 S Douglas Road, 2nd Floor
Coral Gables, FL 33134 USA
info@mango.bz

For special orders, quantity sales, course adoptions and corporate sales, please email the publisher at sales@mango.bz. For trade and wholesale sales, please contact Ingram Publisher Services at customer.service@ingramcontent.com or +1.800.509.4887.

Badass Black Girl: Quotes, Questions, and Affirmations for Teens

Library of Congress Cataloging-in-Publication number: 2019948827
ISBN: (print) 978-1-64250-172-8, (ebook) 978-1-64250-173-5
BISAC category code OUNG ADULT NONFICTION / Social Topics / Self-Esteem & Self-Reliance

Printed in the United States of America

Table of Contents

You Are a True Warrior

"I have a lot of things to prove to myself. One is that I can live my life fearlessly."

—**Oprah Winfrey**, American media executive, actress, talk show host, television producer and philanthropist

Dear Badass Black Girl,

You are a true warrior who inherited the strength, courage, wisdom, love, and dignity of our ancestors. You stand on their shoulders, carrying a history of triumph. Yes, it is true: you also still carry some of the pain of yesterday's Black heroines—these creators, innovators, and agents of change—and you are faced with the tremendous struggle of the modern girl of color. But make no mistake: you are strong and you can conquer whatever challenges this world hands you.

Your very existence defies history. Never forget those who broke the unjust rules society once used to limit their progress, those who fought hard to get you to this moment, those who gave light so others could find the way through dark times. Because of them, you get to walk into a restaurant through the front door, sit at the front of the bus, and cast a vote for leaders who represent your ideals. Walk in the freedom they secured for your sake. Be proud of your rich skin, and may your hair be a crown that stands tall. Be proud of your deep-rooted culture(s). Be proud of the power of those who came before you, as the strength of generations will propel you forward and carry you through difficulties.

Be fearless. But, as you move through the world, remember: your biggest responsibility is to remain thoughtful, to honor where you come from, and to recognize you didn't simply appear and find your own voice. Alice Walker wrote, "How simple a thing it seems to me that to know ourselves as we are, we must know our mothers' names."

Kenbe (be strong),
MJ

You Have a Lot Going for You

"It was when I realized I needed to stop trying to be somebody else and be myself, I actually started to own, accept and love what I had."

—**Tracee Ellis Ross**, American actress, model, comedian, director, and television host

Dear Badass Black Girl,

You think I don't know you, but I do. I see you when your face is stretched by a smile—when you make those around you feel like they are the only people you've ever truly smiled at. But I've also seen your face when you clamp your lips as if you could trap your sadness inside. And there is a story there—beginning, middle, and end—all laid out within the curves of your mouth. I see you with more possibilities than you could ever imagine.

Unless they get in the way of the talents you do have, please don't waste time focusing on the talents you don't have. Don't even seek to improve them (*maybe* later). Don't obsess over your flaws. How many hours will you spend furiously perfecting scales on the piano before you realize playing music is not your *forte*? Not everyone is Hazel Scott or Nina Simone. You don't have to be on the dance team if it's not your thing. You don't have to know the lyrics to the latest Cardi B. or Nicky Minaj song. You don't have to be fluent in Spanish. You don't have to make a mean bread pudding.

Stop trying to be someone else—the girl your friends, your boyfriend, your teachers, or your parents want you to be. Instead, cultivate YOUR strengths. Be YOU. Don't expect your flaws to fall from you like dried-up flakes of skin. If you're not meant to do something, let it go. All your life, you've been told that you need to get better at what you're not good at and don't care about. It may be true that it's good to try new things out, and that we surprise ourselves when we learn something new, but your time is better served when you focus on what you already do well.

You have so many talents. Prioritize them. You may not know exactly what these talents are—and that's okay.

You'll figure it out, and this book will help you.

In the meantime, you don't have to prove yourself to others. You can't dance. So, what? Slow dance, low dance, and fast dance like no one's watching. Do it because the groove hits your spine and moves you in a certain direction. You can't sing? So what? Belt out Beyoncé, croon to Aretha Franklin (R-E-S-P-E-C-T), and swoon to Alicia Keys with all the strength your off-key voice can muster. Play your music loudly, so the bass thumps in your heart and makes your chest feel like it's alive. Because it is.

Kenbe,
MJ

Yeah...You're Awesome!

"Pledge that you will look in the mirror and find the unique beauty in you."

—**Tyra Banks**, American television personality, producer, businesswoman, actress, author, model, and singer

Dear Badass Black Girl,

When you hear the word *talent*, the first image you see might be something artistic or creative—knowing how to play the drums, dance, paint, cook, or create super rad jewelry. What if you're not the creative type or the next Maya Moore on the basketball court? What if you're not like your best friend Deja, whose slender ballerina body moves with a mixture of grace and precision, her hair, dark and soft, swept back in a smooth roll? And what if you really have no idea what you're good at, and you feel like you carry this heavy uncertainty like an extra body, a cloak, or a mask that hides you from the world?

Of course, there are online tests to help you identify your strengths, but there are three no-fail ways to find out what you're awesome at. Don't forget—your best allies are the people who support you and encourage you to excel at what makes you shine.

Kenbe,
MJ

One, Two, Three...Yolo!

A What are you doing well today?

B ASK YOURSELF: What do I do naturally, easily, that feels like fun? It may sound obvious, but how often do you really think about some of your skills, especially the simple ones—organizing your schoolwork or planning the best sleepovers or girls' nights out? Maybe you don't take things personally when people around you are upset, or you know how to keep calm in stressful situations: those are incredible talents. Maybe little kids can't get enough of your funny stories. Maybe your family raves about your apple pie or upside-down cake every time you make it. What do your sisters, brothers, teammates, parents, and the old lady across the hall always call you for help with? What do you have fun doing that seems effortless but other people struggle with? Which of your skills and talents make you the happiest or give you the most pride? Which ones do you most admire in others? Which ones would you like to develop?

D **C** What have you done well in the past?

NOW, TAKE A STEP BACK, and think about five times when you were particularly proud of yourself—whether these successes were small (you were Fortnight's last "man" standing) or totally brilliant (you shined at the National Spelling Bee in Washington DC). What did you do to succeed? What attitudes and behaviors did you use? What similarities exist among these experiences?

E What positive feedback do you get all the time?

F CHANGE THE POINT OF VIEW and ask five people you trust the following question: If you had to rely on me for something important, what would it be? Once they've answered the first question, go further: What makes you think that I could do it? However, ask them to answer positively. We're not doing this to point out your weaknesses. This activity's goal is to reveal your strengths.

Easy Enough?

"Never be afraid to sit awhile and think."

—**Lorraine Hansberry**, Black American playwright and writer

Dear Badass Black Girl,

Through these steps, you can identify what has worked in the past and what you have going for you right now. Based on these successes, you will be more specific about your goals. Of course, nothing is set in stone—circumstances evolve, and people change. But it's a good place to start and gain some insight and peace about the direction you'd like to focus on.

Know also that answering these questions is not always easy, and you might come face-to-face with your own trouble spots and weaknesses. You need to resist the temptation to look at yourself too closely through the lens of other people's strengths. Maybe your friend, Celeste, is carefree and funny. She is *liberated*. Unlike you— so plain, so boring. You're anything but plain or boring. You're just not Celeste.

Girl, stop! Be your own person.

The key is to move forward, and this three-step evaluation helps you do just that.

Kenbe,
MJ

What You're Up Against

In our community, we understand the beauty of multi-generational families, and, if you're like me, you're super tight with your grandparents, your aunties and uncles, and many other members of your extended families.

Many of our Black families are non-traditional in structure. For example, 70 percent of all Black children are raised in single-parent households. And this number gets us a lot of bad press.

The high number of single-parent families in the Black community is caused by many different problems. What do you think some are? How does growing up with one parent or guardian make things different for kid? What kind of community or family support would make it easier for these families to do well?

Google It!

AFFIRMATION: Today is going to be an incredible, beautiful day. Because I am enough. Because I deserve every bit of success I work at to achieve. Because I'm worthy of all my big dreams.

"You're not obligated to win. You're obligated to keep trying to do the best you can every day."

—**Marian Wright Edelman**, American activist for children's rights

8 Badass Trailblazers in Entertainment (1900–1969)

1919 Born in 1896 in Mississippi, screen actress and jazz singer **Evelyn Preer** was the first Black actress to achieve celebrity status. She was nicknamed the "First Lady of the Screen" by her fans in the Black community. Preer starred in the first of her many film appearances in 1919. She was also a talented stage actress who acted in plays by Shakespeare and Oscar Wilde, starred on Broadway, and recorded with notable jazz artists like Duke Ellington. She walked away from a five-film contract with Al Christie Studios after she refused to put on blackface makeup to further darken her complexion.

1934 **Josephine Baker** left the United States for Paris when she decided she'd had enough of performing for segregated audiences. In Paris, she was known to bring her pet cheetah, Chiquita, with her on stage. Chiquita made things even more exciting for audiences by regularly jumping into the orchestra pit to scare the musicians. Baker was the first Black female lead in a major motion picture, *Zouzou*, in 1934. During World War II, she was part of the French resistance to Nazi occupation and was awarded a medal by the French government for her work as a spy. She was such a fierce advocate for Civil Rights that, after the death of Dr. Martin Luther King, Jr., his widow, Coretta Scott King, offered to let her lead the Civil Rights Movement, but Baker refused out of concern for her children's safety.

A wax figure of Josephine Baker is seen on display at Madame Tussauds on December 6, 2013 in New York City.

1940 **Hattie McDaniel** is best known for being the first Black woman to win an Academy Award in 1940 for her role in *Gone With the Wind*. She was also the first Black American woman to sing on the radio in the United States and has not one but TWO stars on the Hollywood Walk of Fame.

A postage stamp printed in the USA showing an image of actress Hattie McDaniel, circa 2006.

1955 **Dorothy Dandridge** was the first Black woman nominated for an Academy Award for Best Actress in a Leading Role for her performance in *Carmen Jones*. The year before year, she was also the first Black woman to appear on the cover of *LIFE* magazine.

A postage stamp printed in the USA showing an image of singer Marian Anderson, circa 2005.

1955 **Marian Anderson** became the first Black woman to perform with the New York Metropolitan Opera and, at the invitation of Franklin Delano Roosevelt, the first to perform at the White House. Anderson's father died when she was only twelve years old, leaving her mother to raise her and her siblings alone in Philadelphia. With no extra money to pay for formal lessons, Anderson was largely self-taught and practiced soprano, tenor, alto, and bass parts for her church choir. Impressed by her vocal range and dedication to singing, her congregation raised five hundred dollars to pay for formal lessons. And that's all it took for Marian Anderson to gain recognition for her talent. Soon, she performed at the Lincoln Memorial and Carnegie Hall and gained fans on both sides of the Atlantic. She sang the national anthem at John F. Kennedy's inauguration and was later awarded the Presidential Medal of Freedom by Kennedy.

1962 **Ethel Waters** became the first Black actress to earn an Emmy nomination for a guest appearance on the "Goodnight Sweet Blues" episode of *Route 66*. She was also the first Black actress to integrate "The Great White Way," as Broadway was known in the 1920s and 1930s, and was the first Black person, male or female, to host her own prime time variety show, *The Ethel Waters' Show*, a fifteen-minute NBC program that aired a decade before Nat King Cole's show.

A stamp printed in the USA shows Ethel Waters (1896-1977), circa 1994

Actress Diahann Carroll at the 33rd Annual NAACP Image Awards at Universal Studios, Hollywood.

1968 **Diahann Carroll** became the first Black actress to land a leading role in the television series *Julia*. Her work on the series brought her the very first nomination for a Primetime Emmy for a Black actress and helped her win a Golden Globe Award for "Best Actress in a Television Series." Her role in *Julia* was notable because it was one of the first television roles with a Black actress who wasn't cast a domestic worker in a white household.

1969 **Linda Martell,** a rhythm and blues and country singer, became the first Black woman to join musician Roy Acuff on the stage of the Ryman Auditorium for the weekly radio broadcast of the Grand Ole Opry in Nashville, Tennessee. At the time, Martell was only the second Black performer (after Charley Pride) to grace the stage of the longest continually running radio program in the United States, which first aired its program in 1925. Martell was also one of the few Black country singers to make a guest appearance on the weekly television variety show *Hee Haw.*

Find more Badass Trailblazers in Entertainment on pages 71, 91, and 140.

What Are You Doing Well?

"Yes, I do have a big ego...and I am in love with myself...because if you don't love yourself, how can anybody love you back?"

—**Mel B.,** English singer-songwriter, rapper, producer, model, television personality, and author.

Dear Badass Black Girl,

Think about what comes easy to you and not to others. If certain tasks or activities seem so easy, maybe you can use them to express one—or more—talent. Do people tell you that you explain things so clearly and are such a good listener that you would make a great teacher? Do they say, "I wish I could do that!" Or "Wow! You did that?" Those are your trigger phrases. The next time you hear them, take note and recognize you are being praised for your secret talent.

When I was a small girl, my parents were very strict with my older sisters—they were not allowed to go to parties, and they hardly ever had friends over to our house. My father was all hard angles—his body could cut you if you got close if you weren't careful, if you didn't know the right way to move around him.

But by the time I turned thirteen, my parents were too tired to police my life. My older sisters had worn them out, and my teenage years became one party after another, not only night after night, but sometimes an afternoon gathering at one house followed by an evening party somewhere else. I danced, sang, and danced, and sang. I wore trendy wide-legged jeans, white denim, neon belly shirts, and dresses with abstract, multi-colored designs. At thirteen, I was running my own show, but parties won't get you far in life.

And partying didn't make me happy. What brought me real joy were the times when I was alone where it was quiet and I didn't have to sing, dance, and be part of a crowd. I loved to sit in my father's study and avidly read Corneille and Racine plays, Tintin comic books, and the adventures of Fantômette, the French teenage crime fighter. I loved the smell of books: Musty, inky—earthy, perhaps. It wasn't just the smell of paper. That smell was mixed with page-turning sweat, the spilled ingredients hastily swabbed off the pages of my mother's Haitian recipe book. The smell of eagerness and my hunger for words. The smell of my world.

So, I became a writer. At school, my teachers loved my stories so much they shared them with the class. Sister Anne-Marie (I went to an all-girls Catholic school) put me in charge of the morning prayer, and I wrote poems to God that made students weep and occasionally rose the hairs on the back of my own neck.

I was good at this.

What makes you happy?

What makes *you* happy? Take a sheet of paper and, without thinking too much about it, write down tasks and activities that bring you joy and satisfaction. (If you're in school, avoid focusing solely on academic life. Think about everything *else* that excites you: your passions or your hobbies.) Then, ask yourself, what *aspects* of each task or activity you particularly like. For example, if you're currently a team leader for an extracurricular activity, what excites you the most? Is it taking the lead on some projects? Or, is it paying attention to your classmates—making sure everyone has a part in the project and can bring their special talents to the group?

It's about identifying what captivates you the most. To do this, focus on what you'd like to do right now, not in ten or twenty years. Imagine the weekend is coming and you have several hours to indulge in your favorite activity. No school deadlines. No social engagements. You can spend hours doing what you want all by yourself. You can forget the world and allow yourself to be (pleasantly) absorbed in one task you find both challenging and fulfilling. If you can find an activity that makes time fly and brings you joy, you're in the zone.

There: You're on your way to finding your talents. If you are in the zone, it is likely that you use one or more of your strengths. The next step is to identify the other skills required by this type of task and sharpen them.

What You're Up Against

Too many Black girls had/have to survive a childhood in neighborhoods where death, drugs, and violence surround us. The most dangerous cities in America (Oakland, Cleveland, Baltimore, and Detroit) have large Black populations in some of the most crime-dense parts of the country.

How can community organizations like nonprofits, churches, charities, youth groups, after-school programs, fraternal organizations, and others focused on furthering education, help reduce crime and find alternatives to violence? How can you get involved?

Google It!

AFFIRMATION: I choose happiness. I choose greatness. I know there's nothing standing in my way that I can't handle. I can do this. The sunrise fills me with energy, and every breath I take fills my soul with ease. However big the mountain, I can climb it. Wonderful things are coming my way. Today, I choose to be confident.

*"Life is very short and what we have
to do must be done in the now."*

—**Audre Lorde**, American writer, feminist,
womanist, librarian, and civil rights activist

10 Badass Trailblazers in Politics and Law (1930–1979)

1872 **Charlotte E. Ray** (1850–1911), was the first Black female lawyer in the United States. She was also the first Black woman admitted to the bar of the District Columbia in April 1872 and the first Black lawyer of any gender to be admitted to practice and argue before the Supreme Court of the District of Columbia.

1936 **Mary McLeod Bethune** became the first Black woman appointed to a government post, when, on June 24, 1936, President Franklin Delano Roosevelt named her Director of Negro Affairs at the National Youth Administration. One of the youngest of seventeen children, born to former slaves, Bethune also opened a boarding school for Black girls, which eventually merged with another school to become Bethune-Cookman College. She served as Vice President of the NAACP from 1940 until her death in 1955.

A stamp printed in the USA
shows Mary McLeod Bethune,
Educator, Black Heritage,
circa 1985

1939 The first Black woman judge in the United States was **Jane Matilda Bolin**. Bolin was also the first Black woman to earn her degree at Yale Law School, the first to join the New York Bar City Association, and, after becoming the first Black woman in the New York City Law Department, became the only (and first) Black female judge in the United States when she was appointed justice in Domestic Relations Court of New York City on July 22, 1939. She remained the only Black female judge in the United States for twenty years.

1947 **Alice Dunnigan** was the first Black female reporter to receive White House press credentials. She was the first Black correspondent to travel with a sitting president when she joined President Harry S. Truman on his campaign tour. In 1947, Dunnigan made history when she became the first Black woman to serve as a White House correspondent.

A stamp printed in the United States, shows Patricia Roberts Harris, circa 2000

1965 **Patricia Roberts Harris** was the first Black American woman to hold two cabinet positions. She was Secretary of the Department of Housing and Urban Development and Secretary of Health, Education, and Welfare during the Carter administration. Harris was also the first Black woman to hold an ambassadorship. She was ambassador to Luxembourg during the Johnson Administration.

1966 **Constance Baker Motley** was the first Black woman to hold a federal judicial post. She was appointed a US District Court judge on August 30, 1966. She also became the first Black woman to argue a case before the US Supreme court when she successfully argued *Meredith v Fair* in 1962, which won James Meredith the right to attend the segregated University of Mississippi.

A stamp printed in the USA shows Shirley Chisholm, Black Heritage, circa 2014

1968 **Shirley Chisholm** was the first Black woman to serve in the US House of Representatives. She ran under the campaign slogan "Unbought and Unbossed" and represented her district in Brooklyn for seven terms from 1969 to 1983. She was also the first Black woman to run for US President, and the first Black woman to take the stage in the Presidential debates in 1972.

1976 **Barbara Jordan** was the first woman of any color to deliver a keynote address at a Democratic National Convention. She was also the first Black of any gender to be elected to the Texas Senate after Reconstruction and the first Southern Black of either gender to be elected to the US House of Representatives.

A stamp printed in the USA shows Barbara Jordan, Black Heritage, circa 2011

1977 **Azie Taylor Morton** was the first Black woman to sign US currency. She was the thirty-sixth Treasurer of the United States and remains the only Black woman to have held that post.

1979 **Amalya Lyle Kearse** was the first woman appointed to the US Court of Appeals and the second Black person of either gender (after Thurgood Marshall). She was named to the Second Circuit in 1979. She is also a world-class bridge player.

Find more Badass Trailblazers in Politics & Law on pages 83 and 171.

What Have You Done Well in the Past?

"There have been so many people who have said to me, 'You can't do that,' but I've had an innate belief that they were wrong. Be unwavering and relentless in your approach."

—**Halle Berry**, American actress

Dear Badass Black Girl,

Go back in time. Give yourself two or three hours. Bring out everything and anything that will help you travel back to the past: old calendars and diaries, photo albums, letters, cards, souvenirs… (You should probably also take out your phone to explore some of your social media shares, but remember to stay focused.) Relax, and look for moments in your life when you have felt a strong positive emotion—pride, joy, satisfaction—after making something verbally, artistically, intellectually, with your hands or physically, that you know (or feel) was the expression of your deep being.

You produced it effortlessly, and it gave you great pleasure.

List these different moments, and find a common denominator: *I animated a group, I prepared a meal, I listened and advised a friend,* etc. Create a Pinterest board, and pin images that symbolize these successful moments. Create another board with skills that are meaningful to you but still need to be sharpened. Commit to work on these skills regularly in order to fully develop your talent.

Kenbe,
MJ

What You're Up Against

Black people are often accused of having a "victim mindset." You might hear things like: "Slavery ended more than 150 years ago, when are you people going to get over it?" and, "Oh, every race has had slaves at some time in history. It's not just Black folks." Then there's, "Did you know Africans were slave-owners before white people?" and, "Who do you think sold Black people to the whites? It was Africans selling off their own people." It's enough to make you want to throw things.

What do you think? Has a victim status become our collective identity? Or is there more to the history than just victimhood? Why is it important to remember that many Black people in the United States (and elsewhere) have a history with roots in slavery? How does that history impact you today?

Google It!

AFFIRMATION: I am amazing. There is no one better to be than who I am right this minute—and I can become who I want to be. Because I am complete, I enrich the lives of my family and friends just by being myself. I am capable of greatness.

"I always believed that when you follow your heart or your gut, when you really follow the things that feel great to you, you can never lose, because settling is the worst feeling in the world."

—**Rihanna**, Barbadian singer, businesswoman, fashion designer, actress, and philanthropist

9 Badass Trailblazers in STEM

1864 **Rebecca Davis Lee Crumpler** was the first Black woman in the United States to earn a Medical Degree and practice medicine. She is also believed to be the first Black American and the first American woman to write a medical book. Her *Book of Medical Discourses* was published in 1883.

1879 **Mary Eliza Mahoney** was the first Black woman in the United States to formally study nursing, earn a degree, and practice nursing as a licensed nurse.

1884 **Judy W. Reed** was the first Black woman to file and receive a US patent. Her invention is called a "Dough Kneader and Roller." No other information exists about her in historical records.

1933 **Ruth Ella Moore** became the first Black American woman to earn a PhD in natural science. She studied bacteriology and taught at Howard University.

1943 **Euphemia Lofton Haynes** was the first Black American woman to earn a PhD in mathematics.

1973 **Shirley Ann Jackson** is the first Black American woman to earn a PhD from MIT and the second Black American woman to earn a doctorate in physics in the United States.

1986 **Patricia Bath** invented the laserphaco probe for cataract treatment in 1986. She is the first Black American to complete a residency in ophthalmology at New York University and the first Black American female doctor to receive a medical patent. Her device enabled surgeons to restore sight to many people who were blind for as long as thirty years.

1992 **Mae Carol Jemison** is an engineer, physician, children's author, and NASA astronaut. She became the first Black American woman to travel into space in 1992 when she served as a mission specialist on the space shuttle *Endeavor*. Since retiring from NASA, she has written several children's books and made an appearance on *Star Trek: The Next Generation* among other television appearances.

2019 **Dr. Venita Simpson** became the first Black woman to complete a Neurosurgery residency at Baylor College of Medicine since the program began in 1956. She's also a Lieutenant Commander in the US Navy.

Find more about Badass Trailblazers in STEM on page 158.

Some Introspection

"Surround yourself with only people who are going to lift you higher."

—**Oprah Winfrey**, American media executive, actress, talk show host, television producer and philanthropist

Dear Badass Black Girl,

Despite my time partying as a teenager, I've always played by the rules. While I spent hours reading Victor Hugo and writing short stories—and brought home the good grades my parents expected—my friends Lola and Estelle snuck into nightclubs and smoked cigarettes on forbidden road trips. They smoked pot together and wore black lace under their school uniforms. I was too boring—a girl who kissed and told. I even sinned and told. We left a store once with Twix bars that hadn't been paid for. I was the one to hike back into the supermarket in the pouring rain, plunk my buck down on the counter, and tell the cashier, "I don't think I paid for this." I had an innocent look about me too. Wide-eyed and sweet.

Now, as a badass Black woman running her own company, these values hold up the foundation of my business: my clients trust me because I am dedicated and honest. It's important to remember that it's never too late to change if you've resorted to cheating in the past. You can make things right for yourself by shifting directions and doing things honestly.

Reconnect with the child in you. Think for a moment about what you liked to do as a child: What games did you like to play? Which activities gave you pleasure? This exercise may seem futile, but it will help you figure out your deepest likes and dislikes. Close your eyes and imagine some scenes from your everyday life, back when you were in elementary school. What gave you the most pleasure? What did you find the most fun? Did you enjoy group activities or prefer to work alone?

These memories are valuable because they help you become aware of your talents and the activities that appeal to you most today. What makes us vibrate as a child is not so far from what captivates us in our teenage years or adulthood. The strengths and talents that underlie these activities are the same, but are simply used in different environments. Next, identify that **one** element that most likely brings you joy during your current activities.

Kenbe,
MJ

Change the Point of View

"Everything is worth it. The hard work, the times when you're tired, the times where you're a bit sad, in the end, it's all worth it because it really makes me happy. There's nothing better than loving what you do."

—**Aaliyah**, American singer, actress, and model

Person	If you had to rely on me for something important, what would it be?	What makes you think that I could do it?
1		
2		
3		
4		
5		

"Never underestimate the power of dreams and the influence of the human spirit. We are all the same in this notion: the potential for greatness lives within each of us."

—**Wilma Rudolph**, African American sprinter

Think About It

What three things are you most proud of in your life right now? | If you only had to do one thing in the time you have left to live, what would that thing be? | **What is your mission in life or the contribution you have to make to the world?** | *What is "no big deal" to you that others struggle with?* | What do you do well without thinking? | **For what tasks or activities do you receive the most compliments and positive signs of recognition?** | *We all have activities that come naturally to us—those things we excel in with little effort or prior knowledge. What comes naturally to you?* | There are too many problems in the world to count, but among all the problems in the world, one thing bothers you the most. What one problem in the world do you want to solve? | **What do you receive praise for that satisfies you the most?** | *What would you do if money wasn't an issue?* | Do you find people often compliment you on skills that seem easy? | **Are there any activities you've performed at school that make you lose track of time?** | *What do you think you can do well but haven't tried yet? Why haven't you gone for them?* | What activities do you finish and think, "I can't wait to do that again"? | **What have you done well without needing instructions?** | *What have other people told you you're great at?* | Think back over your life by starting with your earliest memories. On what have you been complimented? Noticed or rewarded for? What feedback have you received that rang true with you? | **Examine your possessions and what you've collected: books, equipment, memorabilia, treasures, tools, knick-knacks, furniture, etc. Are** there any thematic elements to your most prized possessions? What does this reveal about you? For example, if you collect comic books and art supplies, you might be a great graphic novelist! | *What was the happiest day of your life? Why? What happened that day that affirmed something foundational about yourself?* | Your worst day? Why? What was trampled on? | **What activity (school-related or extracurricular) brings you the most satisfaction?** | *What bores you or makes you feel tired, wooden, and forced into doing it?* | What do you realize or understand more than most people? | **If you could change one thing about the world and what we experience by being here, what would that be?** | *Blogs, ads, YouTube, newsletters, webinars, radio, infomercials, conferences—all of these are good for learning new skills and about the world around you. But how much do you know about what you think? Pay attention to your thoughts. Buy a small notebook, carry it with you, and take notes on yourself: what attracts you, engages you, fires up your heart?* | What does passion mean to you? | **What are you good at, and who will pay you to do it?** | *Where is the overlap between what you're currently doing and what you want to do?* | What are you interested in learning more about? | **What kind of legacy do you want to leave behind for badass girls in the future?** | **What is your unique purpose in the world?** | *What do you want to achieve that brings you joy?* | What do other people tell you you're passionate about? Good at? | **What do you daydream about?** | *What would you do if you didn't have to work?*

Reverse the Trend

"I am a feminist, and what that means to me is much the same as the meaning of the fact that I am Black; it means that I must undertake to love myself and to respect myself as though my very life depends upon **self-love** *and* **self-respect.***"*

—**June Jordan**, Jamaican American poet, essayist, teacher, and activist

Dear Badass Black Girl,

To love yourself is to recognize that you are much more than your flaws; you have qualities that make you unique. Learn to love these qualities, and remember that *you are your best thing*. No matter your size—stick-figure, plus-sized, voluptuous, or muscular, short, very tall—no matter the shape of your curves, the size of your lips, no matter your shade—light or dark, ebony or porcelain-skinned—no matter whether you're quirky, clumsy, shy, outgoing, or anywhere in-between, and no matter the feelings that you have, you must undertake to love yourself. *You are enough.*

You might have learned to be reluctant to talk about your qualities and too often focus on your shortcomings. Let's reverse this trend! Embrace your complications. Know your flaws and weaknesses, but celebrate what's beautiful and strong inside of you too—even if it makes others uncomfortable. It will lead to self-love, self-understanding, transcendence. Never limit yourself because of others' limited imagination. To quote Michelle Obama, lawyer, writer, and former first lady of the United States, "We need to do a better job of putting ourselves higher[…]."

List all your qualities in a notebook. What are you good at? These are important, as they will allow you to deal with whatever life puts before you. And if you're having a hard time figuring them out, remember the compliments and positive messages that you usually receive from your entourage: your parents, relatives, friends, and classmates. What do they say about you? What compliments do you receive regularly?

Write together all your positive traits, talents and qualities on a sheet in your notebook, and don't hesitate to revisit them when you feel low and need a boost of self-esteem.

You are smart.
        You are talented.
                You are badass.

Kenbe,
MJ

What You're Up Against

Research and history tell us that three basic images of Black femininity exist: the Strong Black Woman, the Angry Black Woman, and the Black Jezebel.

"Strong Black Women" are legendary: Harriet Tubman, Sojourner Truth, and every Black grandmother is renowned for her persistence and perseverance. The image of the Strong Black Woman affects how other people see you and probably how you see yourself. While there are many positive aspects of being a Strong Black Woman, this image can also create anxiety and stress. As a Badass Black Girl, you might be pressured to "keep on keeping on" even when you know you should stop. That image is a lot to live up to. This places your mental and physical health at risk.

What are some healthy ways to practice self-care?

Google It!

AFFIRMATION: When anxiety visits me, I can breathe it all away. Feelings are just visitors, and I can choose to invite them in or show them the door. I know that whatever troubling emotions rush through my mind, they will fade away. I am calm and mindful. Everything will be okay. I have faith that everything will work out as it's meant to happen. I am in control. Today is going to be an awesome day.

"Life was neither something you defended by hiding nor surrendered calmly on other people's terms, but something you lived bravely, out in the open, and that if you had to lose it, you should lose it on your own terms."

—**Edwidge Danticat**, internationally acclaimed Haitian American novelist and short story writer

10 Badass Trailblazers in Sports

1917 **Lucy Diggs Slowe** became the first Black American woman to win a major sports title at the very first American Tennis Association tournament. She was also the first Black American woman to serve as a dean of women at an American university.

1948 **Alice Coachman** became the first Black woman to win Olympic gold for the US Olympic team in track and field for the high jump. She was also the first Black American woman to win an international product endorsement deal from Coca-Cola, placing her face on billboards all around the world.

A stamp printed in the USA shows Althea Gibson (1927-2003), tennis player, series Black Heritage, Forever, circa 2013

1956 Multi-talented athlete **Althea Gibson** was the first Black tennis player of either gender to cross the color lines of international tennis. She was the first Black woman to compete at Wimbledon and the first to win a Grand Slam title in 1956 when she won the French Championship. The next year, she won at Wimbledon and the US Nationals. In 1958, she went back and won both of them again. Then, when she retired from tennis, she went on to become the first Black American woman to play on the professional golf circuit! Truly badass.

1960 **Wilma Rudolph** was known as "the fastest woman in the world" and, in 1960, she became the first American woman to win three gold medals at the same Olympic Games in track and field for the US Olympic team in Rome, Italy.

Stamp printed in the United States, shows Wilma Rudolph, athlete, circa 2004

1977 **Cardte Hicks** was the first Black American drafted to play professional basketball, and the first woman to dunk in a professional game. She did it in Holland during a professional MEN'S game.

fl. *1999* **Serena Williams** became the first tennis player to win twenty-three Grand Slam singles titles in the open era.

Serena Williams in action at the 2015 Mutua Madrid Open WTA Premier Mandatory tennis tournament

2012 **Gabby Douglas** became the first American gymnast to win both solo and team all-around gold medals for gymnastics during one Olympic Games. She did this at the 2012 Olympic Games in London. She is also the first woman of African descent of any nationality to achieve this feat.

Olympic champion Gabby Douglas of United States competes on the balance beam at women's all-around gymnastics qualification at the Rio 2016 Olympic Games

2014 **Mo'Ne Davis** was the very first girl to pitch a shutout and win a game in the history of the Little League World Series.

Mo'ne Davis at the 17th Annual HollyRod Designcare Gala at the The Lot on August 8, 2015 in West Hollywood, CA

2017 At Dover International Speedway, **Brehanna Daniels** became the first Black American woman to pit a car in a national NASCAR race.

2019 **Nicole Lynn** became the first Black woman sports agent to represent a top three pick in the NFL draft. She represented Quinnen Williams.

When It Rains, It Pours: Other Strategies to Discover Your Talents

*"Just be honest and true to yourself.
If your friends around you love you,
they'll wish you the best and want only
what's going to make you happy."*

—**Meagan Good**, American actress

Dear Badass Black Girl,

Here are other methods to help you identify and develop your talents so you can fully exploit your potential.

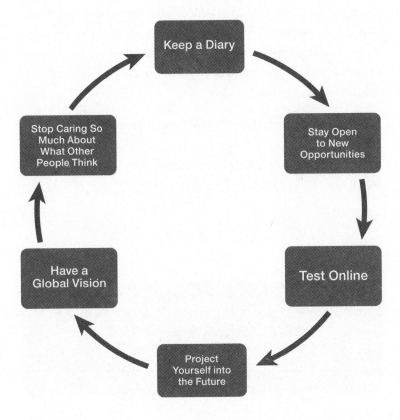

What You're Up Against

If you're the only Black girl on the lacrosse team, you might be teased by family and friends for playing "white" sports. Are you "acting white?" This is a common accusation directed toward Black girls. It has nothing to do with wanting to be white and everything to do with what it means to be Black. In other words, the accusation of "acting white" is perceived as an attack on one's racial identity, which in turn, can create anxiety.

Are there things you enjoy doing that are different than what most of your friends enjoy (whether it's something like lacrosse, ballet, or chess)? How have other people with similar interests (regardless of color) dealt with bullying and being teased?

Google It!

AFFIRMATION: I am free to make many of my own choices, and I give myself permission to choose what works best for me. I choose to be happy right now. I have the power to make all my big dreams come true. I believe in my goals, and I choose to start achieving them today.

"No person is your friend who demands your silence or denies your right to grow."

—**Alice Walker**, American novelist, short story writer, poet, and social activist

5 Badass Trailblazers in Spirituality

New Haven, CT/USA - September 17, 2017 Pauli Murray Residential College Building

1977 The first Black woman to be ordained as an Episcopal priest was **Pauli Murray**. She was also the first woman to receive a PhD in Juridical Science from Yale Law School.

1979 The first Black American woman ordained by the Lutheran Church in America, the largest of three denominations that later combined to form the Evangelical Lutheran Church in America was **Earlean Miller**.

1989 **Barbara Clementine Harris** was the first Black woman and the first woman of any race to be ordained as a bishop in the Anglican Communion (Episcopal Church).

2006 **Merle Kodo Boyd** was the first Black American woman to receive Dharma transmission in Zen Buddhism, meaning she was recognized as capable of being a successor to the religion's lineage.

2009 **Alysa Stanton** was the first Black American female rabbi. In 2009, Rabbi Stanton became the first Black American rabbi to lead a majority-white congregation.

More of These Strategies

"Hard days are the best, because that's when champions are made."

—**Gabby Douglas**, American artistic gymnast

Keep a diary. If you don't already have an idea of what's easy for you, get a notebook. Then, each time you try something new, pause for a minute and ask yourself if it's been fun and easy. Then, write your reflection in your notebook and, like Janelle Monáe says, "embrace what makes you unique, even if it makes others uncomfortable."

Stay open to new opportunities. For a variety of reasons related to our education, where we live, and who we spend time with, some of us have spontaneously developed passions in certain areas of life and others have not. If at first you have trouble finding an area of interest, rest assured: Passion is something that is built, especially through life experience. The important thing is to stay as open as possible to the opportunities available to you so you can figure out your strengths. But remember Madam C.J. Walker's advice:

"Don't sit down and wait for the opportunities to come. Get up and make them."

What You're Up Against

Black girls and Black women in America not only have to deal with the sexism all women face, but we also have to deal with racism, which to many Black women (and men) is a much more serious issue. Perhaps because of this, many Black women tend to feel obligated to put racial issues ahead of gender-based issues. As a result, Black women struggle more with domestic and sexual violence.

According to the National Organization of Women, over 18 percent of Black women report intimate partner violence and sexual assault in their lifetimes. Notedly, that statistic is based on women who DO report their abuse. Because they face untrue biases regarding their sexuality, and because the relationship between the Black community and law enforcement is "fraught with abuse, mistrust, and neglect," Black women are less likely to report their assault than any other group of women in the United States. Many suffer in silence for years, never sharing what has happened to them. The trauma remains unnamed, unknown, and untreated, and the symptoms worsen.

There are many complicated factors that lead to the disproportionate abuse Black women endure. What do you think some of the causes of this are? And what can be done to empower Black women and lower abuse statistics?

Google It!

> **AFFIRMATION:** People come into my life to enrich it and teach me the lessons I need to learn to grow strong. I am blessed by people who love me, respect me for who I am, and want me to succeed. I'm never alone in my struggles. Angels watch over me. I am loved. I deserve every bit of love that enters my life. I matter.

"Service is the rent that you pay for room on this Earth."

—**Shirley Chisholm**, American politician, educator, and author

7 Badass Trailblazers on the Road and in the Air

A stamp printed in the USA showing pilot Bessie Coleman, Black Heritage, circa 1995

1921 **Bessie Coleman** was the first Black American female pilot. Of mixed Native American and African American heritage, Bessie Smith was unable to take the licensing exam in the United States because of discriminatory rules against Native Americans and Blacks in aviation. So, she took up a collection and went to Paris, France, where she earned an international license in 1921. She returned to the United States where she flew in air shows until her death in a plane crash in 1926.

1930 **Bessie Stringfield** became the first Black woman to ride a motorcycle alone across the lower, connected forty-eight states. She took this trip alone eight times and served as the only Black civilian female motorcycle courier for the US Army during World War II.

1978 **Jill E. Brown** was the first Black American woman commercial passenger airline pilot. She flew with Texas International Airlines.

2003 **Vernice Armour**, USMC captain, was the first Black American female combat pilot in the US Armed Services. She flew an AH-1W SuperCobra attack helicopter in the 2003 invasion of Iraq and served two additional tours during Operation Iraqi Freedom. She was also the first naval aviator pilot in any branch of the military!

2005 **Jeanine Menze** was the first Black woman to earn a US. Coast Guard aviator designation.

2007 First known Black American woman to reach both the North and South Poles: **Barbara Hillary**. At the age of seventy-five, this two-time cancer survivor successfully reached the North Pole, and she reached the South Pole at age seventy-nine. Badass!

2008 **Major Shawna Rochelle Kimbrell** was the first Black American woman combat pilot in the United States Air Force. She flew an F-16 Fighting Falcon during Operation Northern Watch in Iraq.

Wonder. Ask. About Big Things. About Little Things.

"I think us here to wonder, myself. To wonder. To ask. And that in wondering bout the big things and asking bout the big things, you learn about the little ones, almost by accident. But you never know nothing more about the big things than you start out with. The more I wonder, the more I love."

—**Alice Walker**, American novelist and Pulitzer Prize winner, in *The Color Purple*

Dear Badass Black Girl,

People who are open to new experiences tend to be happier. According to researchers, learning new things stimulates the brain and our curiosity. So, take an interest in the world around you—the places and activities you've not yet encountered. You will be able to discover new areas of interest, which will make your life vastly more interesting and fun. They say curiosity killed the cat. Not *this* cat.

Be curious. Try not to focus so much on all the things that you're not—and focus on what you could become.

Be curious. Instead of fussing over what you think is wrong about you—find out how to develop your gifts.

We can learn just about anything we set out to learn, and the internet gives us access to information much more quickly and easily than in the past. There are a bazillion sites and blogs where experts and instructors share their knowledge. You want to teach yourself the guitar? Do it! You want to practice a martial art? Look online for a school or association that teaches classes. You want to learn Tibetan cuisine, yoga, or sewing? Check out all the tutorials on YouTube. Do it! So much can happen when you're open to new ideas and have a playful attitude toward learning.

Be curious. Remove other people's expectations and set your own.

Be curious, and you'll start celebrating yourself more. And what's not to celebrate? Look at how badass you are!

Cultivate your curiosity. Soon, you'll find inspiration and knowledge. And whatever brilliant goals you accomplish, you'll do so not in *spite* of being a Black girl, but *because* you are a Black girl.

Kenbe,
MJ

What You're Up Against

Many of the choices of Black girls growing up in America are shaped by a desire "not to become a statistic." An impeccable grind and an unstoppable hustle might help you to outrun the statistical narrative, but it's exhausting. No one wants to be stuck between a rock and a hard place, and it's important to remember that statistics don't tell the story of the individual behind the numbers.

What statistics have you heard that trouble you? How can you avoid becoming one?

Google It!

> **AFFIRMATION:** Today, I am a leader. I'm so filled with love and compassion for others, I can't help but spread it everywhere I go. I will make a difference in other people's lives today even if it's small. My voice and my actions are powerful and meaningful to others. Today, I will stand up for what I believe in.

"Breathe. Let go. And remind yourself that this very moment is the only one you know you have for sure."

—**Oprah Winfrey**, American media executive, actress, talk show host, television producer, and philanthropist

8 (More) Badass Trailblazers in Entertainment (1970–1989)

1970 **Gail Fisher** was the first Black American woman to win a Primetime Emmy Award for Outstanding Supporting Actress in a Drama Series for *Mannix.* She was also the first Black actress to win a Golden Globe Award for her work on the same show, but she didn't just win one Golden Globe. She won two.

1971 **Trina Parks** starred in 1971's *Diamonds are Forever* as Thumper, the first ever Black James Bond girl. A talented singer and dancer as well as an actress, Parks also helped to choreograph the Tony Award-winning Broadway musical, *The Wiz.*

1972 **Vinnette Justine Carroll** became the first Black American woman Broadway director for the musical *Don't Bother Me, I Can't Cope.* She was also the first Black woman to win a Tony Award nomination for directing that musical and remained the only Black woman nominated for a Tony for direction until 2016.

1973 Following Trina Parks' role as James Bond's badass nemesis, **Gloria Hendry** played the Bond girl Rosie Carver in *Live and Let Die* in 1973. She was the first Black actress to portray Bond's love interest. When the film aired in South Africa, which was still under apartheid at the time, all the love scenes between Parks and Roger Moore were edited out of the film.

1982 **Debra Austin** became the first Black American woman to become a principal dancer for a major American ballet company, the Pennsylvania Ballet. She was also the first Black female principal dancer in the New York City Ballet.

Oprah Winfrey

fl. *1984* **Oprah Winfrey** became the first woman to own and produce her own talk show, the highest rated show of its kind of all time. Winfrey is also North America's first Black billionaire!

1983 **Vanessa Williams,** representing New York, became the first Black woman crowned as Miss America. When nude photos were leaked to the press and Williams stepped down, runner-up Suzette Charles, who represented New Jersey and was also a Black American, assumed the title. Three additional Black Americans have been crowned Miss America: Debbye Turner in 1990, Marjorie Vincent in 1991, and Kimberly Aiken in1994.

1987 **Aretha Franklin** became the first Black American woman and first woman of any race to be inducted into the Rock and Roll Hall of Fame.

Aretha Franklin performs at Radio City Music Hall on February 18, 2012, in New York.

Do Away with Fear

"I have learned over the years that when one's mind is made up, this diminishes fear; knowing what must be done does away with fear."

—Rosa Parks, American civil rights activist

Dear Badass Black Girl,

As a teenage girl, I was curious about everything—people, events, ideas—and I was eager to try new things, even if I didn't know what the heck I was doing.

The nuns at my high school in Haiti once organized a spectacular fair—a blur of colors, smells, and sounds. The sky was full of bobbing balloons, which danced around the sunbeams poking through the clouds. Under a flamboyant tree, the hot dog lady covered sausages with mustard, onion, pickles, tomato catsup, and hot *pikliz*—a Haitian condiment made from cabbage and hot peppers. Students wearing dark blue uniforms and white ribbons spent their pennies and dimes on popcorn, peanuts, homemade ice cream, hamburgers, and Styrofoam cups filled with orange soda. They bought deep-fried foods, tickets to shows and athletic tournaments, and enjoyed rides and prizes.

The PTA had arranged to bring a mare named Madame on school grounds, and I wanted to ride, although I'd never seen a real horse up close before. I gently approached the animal, with her long, graceful neck, solid legs, hooves like buckets, and huge chest. Her skin was black, her tail and mane white, eyes dark and wide, and her coat was bright copper. She had white markings on her face and legs. I watched the girl who sat in the saddle and held the reins. It could be me up there. Madame arched her neck proudly and stepped daintily around mud puddles as if afraid of soiling her feet.

The girl jumped off the horse, and it was my turn. Squeezing the last sip of orange soda from a straw, Bernard, Madame's trainer, asked me for the equivalent of five dollars to let me ride. He wore a stylish, hard hat—the kind made for riders, tight-fitting pants, boots, and a light vest.

Madame seemed tense. She laid her ears back flat and squinted her eyes. Uncertain about getting on, I took the reins, reached up, and grasped the saddle's pommel. I wished I had a helmet, along with boots and long pants instead of shorts. My exposed skin would chafe from rubbing, but I wanted to get on the horse. Bernard cupped his hands so he could boost me onto her wide back.

As I mounted Madame, I accidentally kicked her in the flank. Startled, the horse leapt forward, nearly unseating me as she ran blindly into the trees. I tugged desperately at the reins as she settled into a lumbering gallop toward the chapel.

It was a wild ride—branches ripped past my face, nearly sweeping me off the animal's back—but somehow, I held on to the horse as I tried to guide her. I was not big enough nor strong enough to force Madame to stop.

It was a lonely experience, the animal's ribs pressed hard against my thighs. My heart pounded faster than the horse's hooves on the cement. I tried to regulate my breathing, tried to hold this engine underneath me at a steady pace.

Bernard yelled, "Be in control!"

In front of the school chapel, the horse stopped with a snort. Madame reared up and tried to turn around, first to the right and then to the left, but Bernard waited for her, his face melted into a shriveled scowl. The horse resisted and threw her head up, but I hung on, heart in my throat, whispering, "Gentle, gentle."

Bernard calmed her down. I waited a moment, face flushed with heat, sweat streaking across my face, as the whites of my eyes, I imagined, were still bright with the excitement of the wild ride.

During the ride home from the fair, sitting on the scratchy grey seats of my mother's car, looking down at my dirt-crusted tennis shoes, I recalled the ride on Madame—how I feared I'd be scraped off on a tree and fall winded and wounded on the ground waiting for someone, anyone, to come and rescue me.

Under the animal's labored breathing, the thudding hooves, I'd realized that Bernard had assumed I was capable of riding—just like Mother assumed I was strong enough to deal with the mad ride that was my life in Haiti, where there was political turmoil and danger. No one bothered to get me a helmet.

But maybe I was strong and capable.

No. I *was* strong and capable.

Kenbe,
MJ

"In every crisis there is a message. Crises are nature's way of forcing change— breaking down old structures, shaking loose negative habits so that something new and better can take their place."

—**Susan L. Taylor**, American editor, writer, and journalist

10 Tips for Overcoming Fear

Fear is fueled when you listen to it. Fear takes over when you forget that you don't have to listen to every thought that pops into your head or out of the mouths of those around you. Be aware when fear is trying to control you—and identify how it keeps you from growing. Understand the beliefs behind your own anxieties and those of other people. Often, the things that scare us are just illusions. Explore whether fear is popping up because of something that happened in the past under very different circumstances. Get in touch with your senses to stay in the present moment: Light a scented candle. Hold an ice cube with your bare hands. Let a piece of chocolate melt in your mouth. Listen to a meditation or to relaxing music. Look up at the blue sky, and remember where you are right now.

Fear is fueled by inaction. Sometimes, it takes more energy to do nothing when you are afraid to act than it does to jump into the first step toward overcoming what scares you. Think about jumping off a high dive. If you are afraid of jumping, those moments you stand on the ledge with your toes hanging out over the water, feeling every little bounce on the diving board beneath you are terrifying. The moment you let go of your fear and take the leap, all the fear vanishes, and you begin to *experience* rather than *dread*. Take the first step. Right now.

Fear feeds on indecision. When we focus too heavily on the outcome of a choice we need to make, our minds get tricked into taking all kinds of paths that may or may not pan out. Imagine choices are like directions you choose in a maze. If you reach a dead-end, you can turn around and try something new. You don't have to know how every decision you make will work out. Part of what makes life spectacular is the element of surprise.

Fear is fueled by the unknown. When you start to feel fear rise up, give yourself a reality check. Imagine *the worst-case* scenario, and then ask yourself, "How would I handle that?" Then, imagine *the best-case* scenario, and ask yourself, "How would that feel?" If you can handle the consequences of the worst-case scenario and would feel good with the most positive outcome, chances are, it's just fear messing with your mind.

Fear is fueled by self-doubt. Instead of thinking, " This is just impossible!" try telling yourself, "Of course this is possible!" Trust that can do anything you set your mind to. If you don't have the skills to achieve something, you can learn them.

Fear is fueled by negative attitudes. Practice daily affirmations to keep yourself grounded, and talk to people with positive attitudes when you begin to feel doubtful—surround yourself with positive vibes. Look for those who give you good advice. Think, "I can do this!" and "Why not?" instead of "I can't." Don't get trapped into thinking your current situation is all good or all bad. Remember, you are strong and competent. Focus on the good parts of any situation.

Fear is fueled by falsehood. Don't hide from the facts. Look for the truth in your situation. Remind yourself that many of our fears aren't real, and you aren't the only person in the world who experiences fear. We all have them. Don't be afraid to be afraid. Remember that this is just temporary and completely normal. Fear can't hurt you. It just feels like it can.

Fear is fueled by a lack of breath. When you start to feel afraid, pay attention to your breathing. Oftentimes, when we are feeling anxious, we start to hyperventilate. If you catch yourself holding your breath or breathing short shallow breaths, take a moment to focus on your breath. Slow down. Take a big deep breath, and feel your lungs expand, then exhale slowly through your nose and imagine something that makes you smile. If you can manage it, bust out into deep belly laughter. Learn some coping techniques like meditation or yoga. Keeping a journal will help you also. Write down everything that makes you anxious.

Fear is fueled by your need to be perfect. We all want to be perfect and to make as few mistakes as possible, but the truth is, we all screw things up and make a mess sometimes. Embrace those messes and screw-ups. They all come with lessons we don't learn unless we try and fail. Avoid harsh judgments, both from others and from yourself. Remember: Making a mess doesn't make YOU a mess.

Fear is fueled by procrastination. Think of the choices you make in terms of the steps you need to take to complete them. Let's say you have a driving test to pass in the next year, and you are terrified of driving. You won't do yourself any favors by waiting until the evening before the exam to learn how to drive. Take one step today, another tomorrow, and another the next day. Keep things manageable so you don't become overwhelmed when you can't procrastinate any longer.

AFFIRMATION: I am a warrior. I am full of courage and strength. Today, I will keep going, despite my fears. I am safe. I can conquer anything. When I step outside my comfort zone, and allow myself to face challenges, I grow even stronger than I am right now.

What You're Up Against

When they speak their minds, Black girls are often seen as pushy, bossy, and selfish. You will have to deal with or are already dealing with the stereotype known as the Angry Black Woman—an image designed to discredit us and to say that we are overreacting, that we are too sensitive and unreasonable.

Author Brittney Cooper points out that whenever someone weaponizes anger against Black women, it is designed to silence them. Tyler Perry's *Madea* is a classic example of the Angry Black Woman. An Angry Black Woman will "cuss" you out before hearing you out. But there's a lot to be angry about in the world, and for too long, Black women have been expected to sit in the back and keep our mouths shut.

Learn more about this stereotype and how it might affect your everyday life. What are some creative and positive ways you can express your anger?

Google It!

Think About It!

Loud, Aggressive, and Angry?

That Black woman stereotype, among the many harmful misperceptions Black girls face, might have its roots in another problem. Black girls are often seen as more mature and in need of less protection than other students in the same age group. This is known as an *adultification bias*. Because of this, "when Black girls express strong or contrary views, adults view them as challenging authority or, more fundamentally, simply assume a girl's character is just plain 'bad.' " Instead of being heard and understood, Black girls are too often treated like they have an attitude problem or are a threat. Studies have shown this can lead to some serious consequences for Black girls who are brave enough to speak up when they face injustice. For example, Black girls in school are more than five times more likely than white girls to be suspended from school.

Source: Researchers with the Initiative on Gender Justice and Opportunity at Georgetown Law's Center on Poverty and Inequality

"I will not have my life narrowed down. I will not bow down to somebody else's whim or to someone else's ignorance."

—**bell hooks**, American author, professor, feminist, and social activist.

9 (More) Badass Trailblazers in Politics and Law (1980–2009)

U.S. Secretary of State Dr. Condoleezza Rice testifies before the Senate Foreign Relations Committee in Congress.

1985 **Sherian Cadoria** was the first Black woman to earn the rank of Brigadier General in the US Army.

1988 **Juanita Kidd Stout** was the first Black woman to serve on a state Supreme Court. She was named an associate justice of the Supreme Court of Pennsylvania in 1988.

1992 **Carol Moseley Braun** of Chicago was the first Black woman elected to the US Senate.

1992 **Carole Simpson** was the first Black woman to moderate a Presidential debate. She moderated the second debate of the 1992 election.

1992 **Jacquelyn Barrett** was the first Black female sheriff in the United States. Barrett was elected sheriff of Fulton County, GA, in November 1992.

1998 **Lillian Fishburne** was the first Black woman to reach the rank of rear admiral in the US Navy.

In *2000*, **Condoleezza Rice** became the first female US national security advisor of any race, and in 2005, she became the first Black American woman appointed US secretary of state.

2008 California Rep. **Karen Bass** was the first Black American woman to be elected speaker of a state House of Representatives.

2009 **Susan Rice** was the first Black woman to become a United States Ambassador to the United Nations.

What You Could Do Next

> *"Once you know who you are, you don't have to worry anymore."*
>
> —**Nikki Giovanni,** American poet, writer, commentator, activist, and educator

The Clifton Strengths assessment (Gallup Institute)
"Learn the 34 ways to describe what you naturally do best."
www.gallupstrengthscenter.com/

The Character Strengths Survey (VIA Institute on Character)
"Learn your 24 character strengths."
www.viacharacter.org/character-strengths

Talentoday
"Personality is the secret to success in any role. We use soft skills data to help you drive professional success."
www.talentoday.com/en/

Take an Online Assessment. There are plenty of online questionnaires to help you better understand your behavior, your personality, etc. However, avoid rushing on the first tool called "a miracle." The online questionnaires above are credible resources you might want to consider.

Project Yourself in the Future

"It's not your job to be likable. It's your job to be yourself. Someone will like you anyway."

—**Chimamanda Ngozi Adichie**, award-winning Nigerian writer

Dear Badass Black Girl,

Project yourself in the future. We are not confined to the past nor
locked in our present. What we imagine for our futures has the
power to transform our presents. So, in order to identify all of your
talents, turn toward the future. Imagine you have complete freedom
in your schedule and can plan whatever you want for the coming
years. How would you spend your time?

For a long time, I thought I'd become a doctor. I often visited my
orthopedist uncle during his hospital shifts, and I thought if I
became a doctor, the hospital world would become mine. Nothing
stood still in the hospital. The air was riddled with the risings and
fallings of patients' chests as they breathed and with shifting odds of
recovery. There was life, there was death, and nothing was certain
in the hospital's wards. I imagined what my daily routine would
be if I became a doctor. Stretching limbs across the cold steel of an
operating table, I would open people's insides and see parts of them
no one had ever seen, parts of themselves they could only imagine.
I would fix their broken parts, and then, with delicate stitch work,
I would seal them back up. On the bus, people eyed the biology
and botany textbooks I carried. I talked to strangers on the ride—
women with budding baby bumps, men with tobacco breath. They
told me about their headaches, their back pains, and swelling feet.
Telling them I was not yet a doctor didn't stop them.

But then, I projected myself into the future, and I couldn't imagine
doing anything besides writing—not medical textbooks, but short
stories and poems. The medical life was not for me. I must confess
I often skipped Math class in high school, hiding with Sartre or
Agatha Christie under the school's grapevines until Mother picked
me up. I wanted shelves jammed with books and the musty smell of
paper and ink, bindings and glue.

What do you see in your own future?

Whatever it is, *kenbe*.

MJ

When we're not fully engaged, we often tend to put things to the side and seek what interests us. Even when we like something, it might feel overwhelming to tackle it. Just remember: You do not have to do it all at once. Most projects can be broken down in stages. If you like to write, for example, you can start today by launching a blog—all you need is one post. If you want to create clothes, brew your own kombucha, or draw a comic book, just take the first step.

In a perfect world, everyone would be able to use their talents in their preferred way 100 percent of their time. But, in the real word, you need to remain open to opportunities and spaces that allow you to express your talents.

What You're Up Against

Many Black girls report feeling that they always have to be an ambassador for the race, especially in areas where there the Black population is small. Sometimes, it will feel like the weight of Black history is strapped to your back. It's important to know the history of your roots as much as you can, but also important to remember there is no ONE Black history and no ONE Black heritage. Blackness is a rich, diverse, multicultural group of ethnicities that is not limited to one place of origin on the globe. Even if your roots are in Africa, there are hundreds, if not thousands, of cultural groups within Africa you might have descended from. Remember, it's okay to share what you know, but it's not your job to educate anyone.

What are some of the major cultural groups that have contributed to the legacy of Black history?

Google It!

AFFIRMATION: I have everything I need right now. Right now is all that matters. Opportunity is all around me, just waiting for me to take it. I believe in myself and my abilities. I'm okay right now, and I'm going to be just fine no matter what.

"Give light, and people will find the way."

—**Ella Baker**, African American civil
rights and human rights activist

6 (More) Badass Trailblazers in Entertainment (1990–2009)

1994 **Darnell Martin** was the first Black American woman to direct a major studio's movie. She directed Columbia Pictures' *I Like It Like That*.

fl. 1995 **Shonda Rhimes**, best known for the television drama, *Grey's Anatomy,* became the first woman to create three hit shows with more than a hundred episodes each.

Shonda Rhimes at the 10th Annual Governors Awards at the Ray Dolby Ballroom on November 18, 2018 in Los Angeles, CA

2001 **Beyoncé Knowles** became the first Black American woman to win the American Society of Composers, Authors and Publishers Pop Music Songwriter of the Year.

Beyoncé on stage at Rockefeller Center, New York, NY, December 04, 2006

Actress Halle Berry at the Blockbuster Entertainment Awards in Hollywood, 1998.

2002 **Halle Berry** gave an emotional acceptance speech after becoming the first Black American actress to win the Academy Award for Best Actress for her performance in *Monster's Ball*. She thanked Dorothy Dandridge, Lena Horne, Jada Pinkett Smith, and a slew of other Black actresses. She dedicated her Oscar to "…every nameless, faceless woman of color that now has a chance because this door tonight has been opened."

2004 **Phylicia Rashad**, popular from her role as Clair Huxtable on *The Cosby Show*, was the first Black actress to win the Tony Award for Best Performance by a Leading Actress in a Play for her role in the remake of Lorraine Hansberry's *A Raisin in the Sun*.

Phylicia Rashad walks the runway at the B Michael America fashion show during MBFW Fall at New York Public Library on February 18, 2015 in NYC

Anika Noni Rose wears Pamella Roland on the runway at Heart Truth Red Dress Collection show during Mercedes-Benz Fashion Week at Lincoln Center on February 6, 2014 in New York City.

2009 **Anika Noni Rose,** a film and Broadway actress, was the voice actress behind Princess Tiana, Disney's first Black animated princess, in *The Princess and the Frog*.

Keep an Open Mind

"We teach girls shame. 'Close your legs. Cover yourself.' We make them feel as though being born female they're already guilty of something. And so, girls grow up to be women who cannot say they have desire. They grow up to be women who silence themselves. They grow up to be women who cannot say what they truly think. And they grow up—and this is the worst thing we do to girls—they grow up to be women who have turned pretense into an art form."

—**Chimamanda Ngozi Adichie**, award-winning Nigerian writer

Dear Badass Black Girl,

Keep an open mind. In order to widen your vision and acquire a "panoramic" point of view, try the following exercise.

Identify what makes you feel strong.

Think of times when things seem easy, when it feels like you have all the answers, and you totally rock.

Identify the areas in which you spend the most money.

If all your money goes to sports equipment, music, technology, etc., it is likely that this particular area attracts you. It can also mean a way of life or a specific type of relationship that suits you. Look for activities that match the interests that define you.

Remember what you have been thanked for.

...by others, whether at work or in personal relationships. Being a good listener, a supportive friend, a versatile teammate, an organized student, an efficient helper, an honest daughter, etc. Those might seem natural and obvious to you. But these traits are special—they are real talents on you can rely on in the future.

Create Your Own Experience

"It seems like the entire world has intensely specific opinions on how Black women and girls should be. How we should wear our hair, how we should talk, and the volume at which we should do it. The list goes on: how we should dance, who we should date, what kind of music we should listen to, etc. What I love most about being Black is I've been forced from an early age to confront— and later ignore—all these absurd expectations and live life on my own terms, liberated, with zero F*s left to give."

—**Nicola Yoon**, author of *Everything, Everything* and *The Sun Is Also a Star*

Dear Badass Black Girl,

Stop caring so much about what other people think of you. Don't think about what you eat in public. If you are hungry, eat, and eat what makes you happy. If you want anchovy pizza, don't settle for pepperoni just because other people think anchovies are gross. (For the record, I love, love, love anchovies on my pizza. And pineapple.) Don't get your hair permed just to fit in with other girls—or to make boys look at you more closely. Be proud of your waves, curls, and kinks. Don't wear a dress if you're a baggy jeans type of girl. But if you like dresses, wear them. Don't barricade yourself in your room, feeling sorry for yourself, because you have no one to go out with. Create your own experiences. Take yourself out.

And learn to say NO. Often, we feel unhappy because we say *yes* to too many obligations that aren't in our best interests. Your time is important. Think of it as a finite treasure. Say no to those who want to monopolize your time and drain you of energy: Stop doing so much for others instead of doing things for yourself. You can have your own plans, your own goals. Say no to drama—especially when it has nothing to do with you.

Kenbe,
MJ

Think About It

"You can't be hesitant about who you are."

—**Viola Davis**, American actress and producer

Dear Badass Black Girl,

Ever wonder what's been holding you back? Maybe you're hanging out with the wrong friends. Hang out instead with individuals who force you to level up.

Some people will tell you the darnedest things. Tell me: Why are these just wrong?!

"Can I touch your hair?" | "Is that your real hair?" | **"Oh my God, I love your (skin/hair/eyes, etc.)! Are you mixed?"** | *"You're pretty for a Black girl."* | "You're not really Black" | **"I don't see color."** | *"Why don't you cook?"* | "Wow, you speak really white." | **"Why you talk so proper?"** | *"You don't talk Black"* | "You love Beyoncé, right?" | **"Who's your favorite rapper?"** | *"I didn't want to talk to you at first, you seemed angry."* | "Why don't you smile? You're a pretty girl." | **"Why can you say the n-word and I can't?"** | *"How do you feel about interracial*

relationships?" | "Feminism isn't for Black women." | **"Who is Felicia?"** | *"People like you read?"* | "But you're not like other Black girls" | **"Not everything is about race"** | *"Well, I'm basically Black"* | "I wish I could get as Black as you are when I tan" | **"My parents aren't racist, just old-fashioned."** | *"Why is there no White History Month?"* | "Why is hip-hop so violent?" | **"Will you teach me how to twerk?"** | *"But where are you really from?"* | *"That wasn't racist, right?"* | "Shouldn't you see it as a compliment when your culture is appropriated?" | **"Are Beyoncé and Jay-Z getting a divorce?"** | *"Do you wash your hair when it's like that?"* | "I thought all Black girls had butts like Nicki Minaj" | **"Why do Black girls have big booties?"** | *"I bet you have the best singing voice"* | "Do you know how to make fried chicken?" | **"Why are you so aggressive?"** | *"Why do Black girls always have an attitude?"* | "You're my best Black friend" | **"Are your parents still together?"** | *"Aren't all Black people related?"* | "Why doesn't your name sound ethnic?" | **"Is that a weave?"** | *"What is a weave?"* | "Why can't whites say 'white power'"? | **"Are watermelons your favorite fruit?"** | *"Why are most Black people so lazy?"* | "Why do Blacks have their own channels?" | **"I have Black friends. How could I be racist?"** | *"Did you come up from the ghetto?"* | "Why do you laugh when comedians make racist jokes?"

What You're Up Against

Black girls are often expected to meet white standards of beauty. At an age when feeling attractive and fitting in are so important and difficult already, they feel they have to do more work to be "beautiful." Much of that work centers on having (and keeping) "good hair."

Many Black girls don't grow up hearing about bad hair days—they hear about having "bad hair." Hair issues for Black girls are closely tied to feelings of identity, public perception and how you feel about yourself on a day-to-day, core level.

All girls are victimized by a tyrannical beauty industry, but Black girls are the ones with the specific twist of Black girls' hair.

How have beauty standards for Black women changed throughout history? Particularly for hairstyles? How have certain Black hairstyles become a political statement?

Google it!

30 Days of Purpose

Day 1:

What aspects of your life would you like to make changes to?

Day 2:

Right this second, what four things are you thankful about?

Day 3:

What scares you the most?

Day 4:

Are you happy in the house and neighborhood you live in? Why or why not? Where would you most like to live? Don't limit yourself, it could be anywhere in the world!

Day 5:

Where would you like to be in terms of reaching your goals in 6 months? A year? 5 years? 10 years? What are you doing to achieve these goals? Write out a list of the top 10 goals you want to achieve within a year. Make a list of anything that is preventing you from reaching those goals. What do you see as distractions? Are there items on your to-do list that don't need to be? What in the future gives you the most worry?

Day 6:

Which people in your life are most important to you? How many of the people on your list are people you can depend on to support you in tough times?

Day 7:

What are your personal beliefs? What do you want to accomplish most in life? What do you do that sets you afire? what would make you feel more fulfilled than you are right now? When do you feel most at peace with yourself?

Day 8:

What are the words you use to describe yourself? Are they positive or negative? What 10 things do you love most about who you are? Which qualities and talents that you are most proud of require very little effort? Which are your best qualities? If you asked other people to describe you, what words would they use? Why? What do you dislike about yourself? How can you improve yourself? What makes you feel stressed out? What weighs heavily on your mind right now?

Day 9:

What would the perfect day look like to you? What is your dream life? What beliefs hold you back from living that dream life you imagine?

Day 10:

Over the past year, what have you discovered is true today that wasn't a year ago?

Day 11:

What can you start doing today to make your life more easy and less complicated?

Day 12:

If f you could have a talk with anyone, dead or alive, who would it be? Why? Who are your role models? Why?

Day 13:

What is your personal definition of the word "happiness?" What would bring more happiness into your life? Now, think about this one—what robs you of joy?

Day 14:

What have been your biggest changes over the past 5 years? If you could talk to yourself from 5 years ago, what would you tell her?

Day 15:

If there was no chance of failure, what would you do? If money was unlimited, what would your ideal life look like? (Where would you choose to live, what career would you pursue, what kind of family would you build?)

Day 16:

What did someone do recently to make your day better? How can you make someone else's day better?

Day 17:

What life lesson or insight have you gained from a recent challenge? How did going through the darkness and struggle change you into who you are right now?

Day 18:

If you knew today was your last day alive, what would you do differently? If you could pick one message you'd want to pass along after you've died, what would it be? How would you like to be remembered?

Day 19:

Write a profile of the kind of person you wish to be. Create an avatar for this alternate personality. What's are their qualities? Where do they work and live? How do they face difficulties? Write down some ways you can incorporate the qualities your avatar possesses that you don't think you possess.

Day 20:

Write out 5 positive affirmations about yourself. Repeat them daily.

Day 21:

What memory brings you the most joy and satisfaction?

Day 22:

If you could live during another time period, when would you most want to be alive? What kind of life would you have?

Day 23:

Set a 2 minute timer and write down whatever thoughts flash through your mind.

Day 24:

What can you do today to bring you closer to achieving your goals?

Day 25:

What in life is most important to you? Why?

Day 26:

What can you let go of that's holding you back? (Fears, toxic energy, unhealthy relationships)? What bad habits do you need to quit?

Day 27:

Draw or paint a picture of something that makes you happy. You can put it in your journal, or hang it somewhere to remind you to keep your chin up.

Day 28:

In what ways do you neglect yourself? How can you start practicing better self-care starting today?

Day 29:

What fills you with energy and makes you feel most alive? When was the last time you had that feeling?

Day 30:

Make a list of 5 things you want to try this year that will force you to step out of your comfort zone?

"Sometimes, I feel discriminated against, but it does not make me angry. It merely astonishes me. How can any deny themselves the pleasure of my company? It's beyond me."

—**Zora Neale Hurston**, influential author of African American literature, anthropologist, and filmmaker

5 Badass Trailblazers in Literature

Phillis Wheatley (1753-1784) portrait on the frontispiece of her 1773 book, *Poems on Various Subjects, Religious and Moral.*

1773 Born c. 1753, **Phillis Wheatley** became the first published Black American woman poet in the American colonies. Captured in Senegal/Gambia at about the age of seven, Wheatley was raised in slavery by a progressive white family who taught her to read and write and encouraged her to develop her talents. White publishers, however, were so skeptical that an African slave could write poetry that they forced her to undergo an examination to determine if she was capable of authoring her own poems. She passed the exam and got her book published.

Brooks
GWENDOLYN BROOKS | U

A stamp printed in the USA
shows Gwendolyn Elizabeth
Brooks (1917-2000), American
poet, author, and teacher, series
Nobel Laureate in Literature.

1950 **Gwendolyn Brooks** became the
first Black American woman to win a
Pulitzer Prize in Poetry.

1968 **Nancy Hicks Maynard** became the
First Black American woman reporter hired
by the *New York Times.* She also became
the first Black woman to own a newspaper
(with her husband) when she purchased
the *Oakland Tribune* in 1983.

Toni Morrison, a Nobel Prize-
winning American author, editor,
and professor on May, 12, 2009
in Paris, France

1993 **Rita Dove** became the first Black US Poet Laureate.

1993 **Toni Morrison** became the first Black American woman to win a
Nobel Prize for Literature.

Go Be Brilliant!

"I realized that beauty was not a thing that I could acquire or consume, it was something I just had to be."

—Lupita Nyong'o, Kenyan-Mexican actress

Dear Badass Black Girl,

You will understand—and, I hope, directly observe after you try one or more of these exercises—that we all have many talents. Relying on these talents boosts your motivation and allows you to be happier and more satisfied with life: you gain self-confidence and better define YOUR true value so that you can accomplish whatever brings meaning to your life.

Rather than focusing on your flaws, rely on your talents. You are strong. You are unstoppable. Realizing these facts is a major step toward realizing your full potential. To quote actress, comedian, and writer Phoebe Robinson, "I like the tenacity and creativity of Black [girls], which has been underestimated. People are slowly realizing how wonderful and fully dimensional Black [girls] are—but we already knew that!"

Kenbe,
MJ

What You're Up Against

A lot of Black girls code-switch. They use the vocabulary, intonation, and articulation deemed proper in a "white space" ("How do you do?") and only let their guard down around friends and family ("How's ya day goin'?"). Some of this is natural. No one talks to the principal the same way we talk to a close friend.

But it can be exhausting.

Code-switching is a skill learned out of necessity—not choice. Writer Maya Lewis, for instance, began code-switching when teachers reprimanded the way she spoke, and she decided to hide a piece of herself when she saw how non-Black people responded to her differently ("positively") whenever she added back the "g's" to her words and dropped all slang. It's not uncommon for Black girls to feel like they have to make others feel comfortable when they're in a group (especially if that group is made up of people who look nothing like them). They "dim their light" because they feel they cannot be their true selves without sticking out like a sore thumb, and being set aside.

In school and workplace settings, Black girls are often taught they have to be twice as good to go half as far, as they represent the race and are watched more closely than others. These beliefs are not necessarily inaccurate. However, coupled with the Strong Black Woman image, they run an increased risk for social anxiety.

Where have you seen prominent Black people code-switching in the media? What are some reasons a leader would choose to code-switch?

Google it!

AFFIRMATION: Every day, I take one giant step closer to reaching my goals. I can do anything I set my mind to. I am open to new possibilities and eager to learn as much as I can. I have everything I need right now. I'm doing my best. If I fall, I'll get back up and keep trying. I can do better next time.

"All anyone can hope for is just a tiny bit of love, [...] like a drop in a cup if you can get it, or a waterfall, a flood, if you can get that too."

—**Edwidge Danticat**, internationally acclaimed Haitian American novelist and short story writer

7 Badass Trailblazers in Education

1858 **Sarah Jane Woodson Early** became America's first Black female college professor. She joined the Wilberforce College faculty in 1858.

1862 **Mary Jane Patterson** made history when she graduated in 1862 from Oberlin College with a Bachelor of Arts Degree, becoming the first Black American woman to earn a degree from that school.

1869 **Fanny Jackson Coppin** became the first Black American female school principal at the Institute for Colored Youth.

1883 **Hortense Parker** is the first known Black American woman to graduate from one of the Seven Sisters colleges. She earned her degree at Mount Holyoke Seminary, now Mount Holyoke College.

1920s **Sadie Tanner Mossell Alexander** was the first Black American woman to earn a PhD in Economics in 1921 and the first woman to earn a law degree in 1927. She earned both of her degrees at the University of Pennsylvania.

1968 **Elizabeth Duncan Koontz** was the first Black American woman elected President of the National Education Association in 1968.

1999 **Shirley Ann Jackson** was the first Black American woman university president in the United States. She rose to the President's office at Rensselaer Polytechnic Institute in Troy, New York.

Embrace Your Imperfection

*"What do I love about being Black?
Everything. Every. Single. Thing."*

—**Susan Kelechi Watson**, actress, *This Is Us*

Dear Badass Black Girl,

Honey, you're not perfect. I'm sure you know it. But *embrace* it. You have weaknesses—like everyone else. You'll make mistakes—like everyone else. You'll have a shitty attitude sometimes and say or do the wrong thing. You'll hurt people around you. On some days, you'll even look like crap, and you'll find it difficult to love yourself. You'll feel shame.

And you know what? That's okay. Be happy to be alive, to be able to read this book, to have a conversation about it, to feel a ray of sunlight on your skin, to listen to the breeze move through the leaves of a tree.

While it's not going to help you to focus on your flaws too much, it does help to do a little self-examination and see what you can improve, so you can feel better about yourself when you do screw up (as we all do). Self-compassion boosts self-confidence.

Don't hide from your flaws and pretend you only have positive qualities and talents. Otherwise, how do you expect to evolve? Ask yourself: *Are my shortcomings getting in the way of my talents?* If the answer is yes, well…do something about it! American writer, feminist, womanist, librarian, and civil rights activist Audre Lorde wrote, "Only by learning to live in harmony with your contradictions can you keep it all afloat."

Take the time to list your flaws in a notebook. If you have trouble, think about people around you and what they often blame you for (but I'm pretty sure you can create this list on your own more easily than your list of positive qualities!).

What area did your self-evaluation point at?

Now, ask yourself: How could you minimize these flaws—for the sake of allowing your talents to flourish? For example, maybe you're part of a solid group of friends who want to become the new Spice Girls, but you cannot seem to earn above a D on your school report cards unless you spend extra hours on homework and miss singing practice. What can you do to remedy the situation? What can you do differently to catch up with schoolwork? Maybe instead of painting your nails during study hall as you usually do, you could find a study partner and buckle down. Then, you can make practices AND keep your grades up.

A healthy self-esteem allows us to put our troubles into perspective. When you love yourself, you recognize your struggles and accept them. This doesn't mean you accept failure as the only outcome. It means looking at yourself without judgment and finding ways to work around your challenges. It means finding ways to grow into the person you want to become instead of giving up and going home because some things are a little harder for you.

Use your flaws as a springboard for change. Everything "modifiable" can be transformed into something beautiful. It will become a goal to achieve. For example: "I can't keep up with my jogging partner" becomes "I'm going to exercise more and learn to eat well." If you're not happy with your limited French vocabulary, take a class. Thrive on obstacles. If people say something can't be done, then push harder.

A Black girl with healthy self-esteem understands the difference between the judgment she makes on herself, and the assessment of her skills. For example, you may have a fairly good self-esteem and aware that your grammar skills are atrocious. A healthy self-esteem allows for a more complex (and fairer) vision of yourself. It allows you to embrace your imperfections. Close your eyes. Feel the difference between the two words *accept* and *embrace*. An embrace is kinder. It's the hug you give yourself when you say, "It's okay. No one is perfect."

Have you ever noticed we put up with much more from our friends than with ourselves? We make excuses for our friends—we forgive their flaws, and we cheer them up when they feel like failures. But God forbid we're faced with our own limitations: we feel worthless and often ashamed of ourselves. Celebrate the person you are today: Give yourself permission to come as you are. No change, no masks, no role, no excuses. Value both your strengths and weaknesses.

Embrace your imperfection as you would an old friend.

Kenbe,
MJ

What You're Up Against

Researchers found that when a group is shown photos of different people, Black women's faces were least likely to be recognized out of a group of white men and white women. Statements made by Black women in group discussions were also least likely to be correctly attributed to them than statements made by Black men, white women, and white men. Black women in leadership positions are also more likely to be criticized or punished when making mistakes on the job.

The pay gap for Black American women is also a huge problem in the United States. A 2019 study conducted by the National Partnership for Women and Families found that, on average, women earn 80 cents to every dollar earned by white men. Black women, however, tend to have even lower earnings, on average, bringing in 61 cents to the dollar that white men typically earn.

A number of factors lead to the pay gap many Black women experience, but there are a number of ways you can keep from falling into the pay gap when you become a career woman.

What are some of the reasons for the pay gap? How can you ensure you are paid fairly for your work?

Google it!

AFFIRMATION: I accept myself as I am right now with all my flaws. I don't have to be perfect to shine. I will be kind to myself when I'm weak or make a mistake, but that doesn't mean I'm satisfied. I can be brave and try to do better. I won't give up. I will keep moving forward and face the unknown despite any doubt or uncertainty I feel. I have the right to feel happy and fulfilled.

"You may encounter many defeats, but you must not be defeated. In fact, it may be necessary to encounter the defeats, so you can know who you are, what you can rise from, how you can still come out of it."

—**Maya Angelou**, American poet, singer, memoirist, and civil rights activist

7 Badass Trailblazers in the Military and Government Services

Navy Vice Admiral Michelle Howard arrives at the 44th NAACP Image Awards at the Shrine Auditorium on February 1, 2013 in Los Angeles, CA.

fl. *1818* **Molly Williams** became America's first female firefighter by working with New York's Oceanus Engine Company starting in 1818. Williams was the slave of a wealthy merchant who was a volunteer for the Oceanus Company. When an influenza epidemic broke out, and many of the men were too ill to respond to calls, Williams stepped in. She became known as Volunteer 11 and was known as effective as any of the men in her fire station at fighting fires.

1866 **Cathay Williams** was the first Black female to enlist in the US Army. At the time of her enlistment, women were not allowed to serve, so she signed up under the assumed name "William Cathay." She served for two years until complications from smallpox led a military physician to discover that she was female. She was discharged from the Army in 1868.

1895 "Stagecoach" **Mary Fields** became the first Black American woman to hold a star route delivery contract with the United States Postal Service.

1977 **Carolyn R. Payton** became the first Black American and first woman appointed Director of the US Peace Corps when she was appointed to the position by President Jimmy Carter.

2009 **Lisa P. Jackson** became the first Black American to be named Administrator of the Environmental Protection Agency. She was appointed to the position by President Barack Obama.

2014 First Black American woman four-star admiral: **Michelle J. Howard**. She was the first woman to rise to the rank of four-star admiral in the US Navy. Howard was also the first Black American woman to command a US Navy ship, the *USS Rushmore.* When she retired, she was serving as both commander of US Forces in Europe and as the commander of US Forces in Africa. She was the first woman to command operational forces for the US military.

2018 **Lorna Mahlock** became the first Black American woman to hold the rank of Brigadier General in the United States Marine Corps.

Use Your Mistakes to Grow and Flourish

"We may encounter many defeats, but we must not be defeated."

—**Maya Angelou**, American poet, singer, memoirist, and civil rights activist

Dear Badass Black Girl,

Learn to be okay with your mistakes. Don't let them block your efforts to become your best version of yourself. Instead, allow every mistake, every shortcoming, every failure to become a source of inspiration to do better and a chance to learn new lessons in life. Remember: If you don't learn to fail, you will fail to learn.

When things don't work out, tell yourself:

1 Remember some of your successes. Nobody is a "total loser."

2 Now, think about a particular mistake. While giving yourself permission to feel crummy for a little while, ask yourself: *What lesson can I draw from this experience?*

3 What steps can you take to correct the situation? If you said something stupid on a group chat, apologize. If you're the one who accidentally spilled Clorox on your sister's favorite blouse, acknowledge your mistake, and replace the shirt if you can.

4 Now, imagine yourself in the future when this mistake no longer matters: You have grown from the experience. How much did it *really* impact your life? How do you feel?

Narcissist Much?

"Mistakes are a fact of life. It is the response to the error that counts."

—**Nikki Giovanni**, American poet, writer, commentator, activist, and educator

Accepting our own shortcomings requires a lot of work and energy. You'll have to be courageous and indulgent. You'll have to find the middle ground between *narcissism* and *self-reliance*.

Narcissism is an exaggerated admiration of and focus on oneself. Narcissists believe they are so beautiful and so talented in comparison to others that they are special and deserving of different treatment than others. Narcissists often rely on the admiration of others for their self-worth and seek to be seen as special to other people. They tend to be selfish and make themselves the center of the world. There is a saying, "Cutting off someone else's head doesn't make you look any taller." Narcissists don't understand that. They tend to highlight the failures of others to provoke feelings of inferiority and guilt, especially in those who challenge them or question their attitude.

Self-reliance values success through hard work and experience. It's easier for a girl who's self-reliant to acquire self-compassion and a self-worth that comes from herself and not others. She learns to know herself, to understand herself, to accept herself as she is—which allows her to extend that selfless love to others. She is caring toward those around her, as she doesn't feel the need to belittle others to develop her own self-esteem. She doesn't need others to champion her. She understands this quote by South African activist and writer Malebo Sephodi: "The voice of a Black woman should always be HERSELF… No edits. No erasure. No pressure. No expectations. No additions. No intruders."

Learn to love yourself without falling into narcissism.

Think About It: Where Are You Now?

"I'm not ashamed of what I am and that I have curves and that I'm thick. I like my body."

—**Alicia Keys**, American musician, singer, and songwriter

Dear Badass Black Girl,

Are you too critical with yourself, judging yourself too harshly? Do you regularly compare yourself to others and feel what they are doing or how they are doing it is better than yours? On the flip side, do you know how to keep motivated and congratulate yourself?

Self-love starts with figuring out where you are. *So, where are you right now?*

YES or NO?

	Yes	No
When you look at yourself in a mirror, do you find that you are imperfect but still pretty?		
When you make a mistake, do you take the time to put things in perspective? For example, you could say, "It does not matter. I'll do better next time."		
Do you know your strengths and do all you can to use them to your advantage?		
Do you rarely compare yourself to others?		
Do you seek others' feedback only to learn from it without allowing their words to ruffle your feathers?		
Do you know when to say, "No" when you are asked for too much?		

If you've answered *yes* to all these questions, you've made it a priority to accept yourself for who you are. You trust yourself, know who you are and what you want, and don't allow others to determine your self-worth.

If you've answered *no* to most questions, you might want to complete some of the exercises on the next pages. They will help you learn to love yourself a little bit more, so that you can live a more meaningful life—one in which you flourish academically and professionally, cultivate real friendships, find love, and just feel good about yourself.

What You're Up Against

Black girls often feel like they are pretending. They sometimes feel like imposters when placed in positions of power. That shouldn't come as a shock to anyone, considering how Black women are often treated when they are placed in a position of authority or achieve a difficult goal.

First Lady Michelle Obama had to deal with racists who referred to her as an "ape." Remember when Gabby Douglas became the first Black female Olympic gymnast to receive an all-around Olympic gold medal? Instead of focusing on her achievement, the press and social media went off on her hair style, criticizing her because they claimed it was "unkempt." (Try flipping end over end without mussing your hair!) Some of the shade she received came from Black people.

The truth is, people get jealous when they see others doing well. There's not much short-term work that can prevent this kind of attack. Why do you think Black women in power are subject to unfair ridicule?

Google it!

AFFIRMATION: I am wonderful and beautifully made. I am perfect just the way I am. I'm grateful for my body. I only compare myself to myself, because there's no one else quite like me.

"I didn't have anybody, really, no foundation in life, so I had to make my own way. Always, from the start. I had to go out in the world and become strong, to discover my mission in life."

—**Tina Turner**, internationally recognized singer, songwriter, and actress

4 Badass Trailblazer Activists

Nobel Award-winner Wangari Maathal on a Burundi Stamp

1949 **Florence LeSueur** of Boston's NAACP chapter became the first Black woman president of a chapter in the organization's history.

1955 On March 2, 1955, **Claudette Colvin**, who was just fifteen years old at the time, was arrested for not giving up her bus seat to a white person in Montgomery, Alabama. **Rosa Parks** was arrested in December of the same year for her act of peaceful resistance, several months after Colvin's arrest.

2004 **Wangari Maathai**, a Kenyan political activist and environmentalist became the first African woman to receive the Nobel Peace Prize for her "contribution to sustainable development, democracy and peace." She earned her Bachelor's Degree at Benedictine College in Kansas and her Master's Degree at the University of Pittsburgh in Pennsylvania.

You Rock on a Phenomenal Level

"I realized that I don't have to be perfect. All I have to do is show up and enjoy the messy, imperfect, and beautiful journey of my life."

—**Kerry Washington**, American actress

Dear Badass Black Girl,

Some girls want to be happy. They want to accept who they are—eventually. But they think, *Later, when I'm more beautiful. When I get a haircut. When I lose the weight. Later, I will have more confidence. Later, I will be a better me. I will accept myself when I am organized. But now, I am not enough. I am not pretty enough, I am not competent enough.* Our future self always seems worthier.

What about being happy NOW?

You'll never reach a point where you can say, "I'm perfect." As soon as one goal is reached, another one shows up, demanding your attention. So waiting until you're "better" to enjoy life is like saying "never." Think about death: What are the things you will regret? Personally, on my death bed, it would surprise me if I said: "I regret so much not having had a flat stomach."

While it's good to want to be better and to have ambition, what about showing some love to our present self—and start rocking on a phenomenal level?

Kenbe,
MJ

How to Embrace
Your Imperfection

"It's not the load that breaks you
down, it's the way you carry it."

—**Lena Horne**, American singer, dancer,
actress, and civil rights activist

Dear Badass Black Girl,

American actress, poet, playwright, screenwriter, journalist,
and civil rights activist Ruby Dee writes, "The kind of beauty
I want most is the hard-to-get kind that comes from within—

strength, courage, dignity." But when Black girls think about their imperfections, they often focus on their bodies.

To gain self-confidence and to love one's body is not always easy. Here are five exercises to learn to embrace your imperfection.

Think about the "history of your body"

Write about factors—during childhood, adolescence, and maybe early adulthood—that might have shaped the way you view your body today. Did people make negative comments about your face (Gross! Acne!) or your hair ("I wish you had 'good' hair")? Did your friends make fun of you? Have you allowed the media to tell you how you should look? Understanding where your internal suffering came from is a good starting point for learning to accept yourself as you are and move forward.

Create a hierarchy of your values

When we focus on our bodies' imperfections, we forget that our physical traits should not be a priority in our lives. Think about everything that really matters: health, love, family, friends, fulfillment at work, passions…and put your physical appearance in its right place among all these values.

Accept compliments

When you get a compliment, simply say, "Thank you." No need to add, "Oh, that was easy" or "You really think so?" or "Actually, I think…" Keep these compliments in mind or, better yet, write them down in a notebook and think about them every time you need a confidence boost.

Don't hide your flaws

Changing habits requires time, patience, and (a lot of) courage, but the results are worth it. Start by choosing not to hide your "imperfections" when you are alone at home—then, slowly unveil these flaws when you're with friends or people you trust. Do you wear loose clothing to hide your belly? Change this by choosing tops of a different size and color. And at each stage, congratulate yourself for your courage. Eventually, you'll realize that your flaws are not flaws at all.

American poet, writer, commentator, activist, and educator Nikki Giovanni writes, "A lot of people refuse to do things because they don't want to go naked, don't want to go without guarantee. But that's what's got to happen. You go naked until you die."

Fight it!

Whenever negative thoughts invade you, they cause you to act differently to cover them up, or worse, to give up. Feeling ugly? You use makeup to hide your face. Feeling like a sack of potatoes? You lose all motivation to exercise. Identify all the behaviors you adopt when you feel imperfect. Write them down in a notebook and learn to recognize when the self-criticism cycle begins. What could you do instead? Replace the negative habits with positive ones.

I hope these mental exercises help!

Kenbe,
MJ

What You're Up Against

Black girls not only have to deal with racial bias, but they also have to deal with discrimination based on skin tone. Colorism, or *shadeism*, is a nasty form of prejudice or discrimination where people are treated differently based on how dark or light their skin tone is. People with light-toned skin are treated with preference over dark-skinned people, sometimes even within the same families.

Because of this bias, many dark-skinned Black girls (and dark-skinned girls around the world from many different cultures and ethnicities) try to lighten or *whiten* their skin by applying chemicals to try to remove melanin. This process is also known as *lightening, brightening, depigmentation*, or *bleaching*. Some of the chemicals used in these processes, including mercury, are dangerous, and can cause serious health problems.

Where does this bias against dark skin come from? What is being done to fight it?

Google it!

AFFIRMATION: Today, I will choose to think positively. My positive thoughts create positive feelings, and positive feelings lead to positive actions. I can get through anything that comes up. I am brave and confident. I am strong. I can do anything I set my mind to do.

"If you don't like something, change it. If you can't change it, change your attitude."

—**Maya Angelou**, American poet, singer, memoirist, and civil rights activist

3 (More) Badass Trailblazers in Entertainment (2000–Now)

Issa Rae arrives for the *Little* premiere on April 08, 2019 in Westwood, CA

fl. *2011* **Issa Rae** became the first Black woman to create and star in a premium cable series. She is the creator and star of HBO's hit series, *Insecure*.

2014 **Ava DuVernay** became the first Black woman to direct a film nominated for a Best Picture Oscar—*Selma*. She is also the first Black female director to win the director's prize at the Sundance Film Festival in 2012.

2014 **Quvenzhané Wallis** made history as the youngest actress ever to receive a nomination for an Oscar for Best Actress for her role as Hushpuppy in *Beasts of the Southern Wild*. She also made history when she became the first Black actress to play the lead role in *Annie* in the 2014 motion picture remake.

The Badass Black Girl's Movie List

Year	Title	Rating	Director
2019	*Selah and the Spades*	NR	Tayarisha Poe
2019	*Premature*	NR	Rashaad Ernesto Green Zora Howard
2018	*Jinn*	PG-13	Nijla Mu'min
2018	*Solace*	NR	Tchaiko Omawale
2017	*I Am Not a Witch*	NR	Rungano Nyoni
2013	*Belle*	PG	Amma Asante
2011	*Yelling to the Sky*	NC-17	Victoria Mahoney
2009	*Mississippi Damned*	TV-MA	Tina Mabry
2000	*Love & Basketball*	PG-13	Gina Prince-Bythewood
1998	*Down in the Delta*	PG-13	Maya Angelou
1997	*B*A*P*S*	PG-13	Robert Towsend
1994	*Crooklyn*	PG-13	Spike Lee
1994	*Alma's Rainbow*	NR	Ayoka Chenzira
1991	*Daughters of the Dust*	TV-PG	Julie Dash
1975	*Mahogany*	PG	Berry Gordy

Come as You Are

"A great figure or physique is nice, but it's self-confidence that makes someone really sexy."

—**Vivica A. Fox**, American actress, producer, and television host

Learn about these NOW!

Focus Your Attention

"Dear Exquisite Black Queen…You are original, unique, and exquisite! Embrace your imperfections with confidence and self-love. Your authentic self is your best self! Flaws and all, you're still a rare gem! Black woman, you are phenomenal, please believe that!"

—**Stephanie Lahart**, author, poet, motivational speaker for at-risk teens, and teen mentor

Dear Badass Black Girl,

Don't allow yourself to overthink and dwell on problems you can't act on right now.

I used to take the bus every morning from Miramar to Miami, Florida, where I worked as a court interpreter. While in transit, I often noticed that most people cannot start their day without reading the latest news on their phones or tablets. Wars, famine, political chaos—those are very real, and the fact that these problems pull at your heartstrings says a lot about your kindness. But much of what people see in the media is sensationalized to draw attention, and it can create a lot of anxiety that doesn't solve the problem and isn't healthy for you.

Do what you can: If you want to help the victims of famine, and can afford to do so, make a regular donation to Action Against Hunger. If you can't afford to gift your money, gift your time. Volunteer at a local soup kitchen, animal shelter, or hospital. Those are both actions that can make a difference.

But remember that you cannot always intervene and, even if you could, you couldn't possibly solve all the world's problems. If you already donate to or volunteer for a good cause regularly, take a break from bad news and the misery of the world—or select only information that is useful to you. Use that time to read a good book or magazine, listen to your favorite music, look out the window, and focus on your surroundings. Look for **joy**, an emotion you can create or find even in some of the unhappiest circumstances. It can be anywhere: in the beauty of the sky, in a Beyoncé song, or a conversation with the quiet girl on the bus.

At any moment, you can choose whether you are going to be optimistic or stress out, whether you are going to be relaxed or disturbed, whether you are going to act or convince yourself it's hopeless. The choice belongs to *you*—all the time. I invite you to take two or three minutes to breathe calmly. Close your eyes, relax your shoulders, and remind yourself that every day is the right day to create joy and embrace gratitude. Your determination to create joy, whatever the circumstances, will lead you to freedom: If you want to be sad, no one in the world can bring you joy. And if you decide to be joyful, nothing and no one on Earth can take away that joy.

Kenbe,
MJ

What You're Up Against

Racism traumatizes Black women (and men) in greater numbers than it does other minority groups. This kind of trauma can be directly or indirectly experienced. Examples of direct trauma include driving while Black, shopping while Black, and many other everyday racial micro-aggressions.

But Black people also face indirect trauma by witnessing racist violence against others, often through viral videos, like the ones of unarmed Black women and men being killed that have become commonplace on the internet. Just witnessing race-based trauma can have effects that are nearly as devastating as the direct form.

We can't always avoid the videos that pop up on our newsfeeds on social media sites, but we can educate ourselves about the effects of racism on our mental health and learn some coping mechanisms to minimize how much we are affected by violence in society.

Google it!

AFFIRMATION: Today is going to be a great day. I am happy. I am blessed. Great things are coming my way.

"Whatever we believe about ourselves and our ability comes true for us."

—**Susan L. Taylor,** American editor, writer, and journalist

Reasons to Love Being a Black Girl

Black is beautiful | the strength of generations | **our brilliance** | *our strength and vulnerability* | our sassiness and rhythm | **our strength and resilience** | *Black girl grit and sisterhood* | our courage, wisdom, and love | **cocoa skin** | *natural curls* | we're a tribe | **our depth, breadth, beauty, and brightness** | *we triumph over adversity* | our rich perspectives | **our natural strength and poise** | *our aptitude for activism* | our unparalleled elegance | **shoulders squared and heads up high, even in the face of oppression** | *no matter what, we survive and thrive* | our power and knowledge | **we're proud, strong people** | *our deep-rooted culture* | our collective sense of humor | **Black is movement** | *our sense of community* | our unparalleled joy | **our innate sensibility** | *we're so lit all the time* | we're beautiful and determined | **the strength and power in our DNA** | *our unbreakable spirit* | we defy expectations | **we lift each other up** | *we're sound and versatile* | we're beautifully and colorfully complex | **we're powerful, multifaceted** | *our collective perseverance and strength* | the language of our rhythm and music is universal | **our brilliance** | *we innovate and overcome* | we break through boundaries | **our strength, courage, and determination** | *we're trendsetters and taste-makers* | Black is IT | **we're a multitude, not a monolith** | *we're expansive in our thoughts, interests, creativity, and actions* | that there is no one way to live out my Blackness | **Black Girl Magic** | *we're fabulous* | we are creators | **our skin glows bright** | *we wear color, patterns, and texture* *with style* | we rock hairstyles like crowns | **our history of triumph, perseverance, and dignity** | *we are true warriors* | our strength | **we create some awesome, rad sh*t** | *we are demanding* | we believe in our own dignity | **the tenacity and creativity of Black women** | *our dance moves* | our resilience | **we're so talented, passionate, gifted, magical, and beautiful** | *we embody a myriad of colors, cultures, wisdom, struggles, experiences, and joy by just existing, and we do so with pride* | we're "powerful beyond measure," as the Maya Angelou quote goes | **we transcend anything this world throws at us** | *Black is UNITED* | we celebrate our beauty together | **we have skin that glistens and caramelizes in the sun** | *we change narratives and build nations* | strong and beautiful | **we keep an eye out for one another** | *the gift of being loud (because quiet doesn't always get the job done)* | we're creators and originators | melanin is a gift from God | **we're the mothers of humanity and the heroes of the American nation** | *our hair is a crown that stands tall* | Black is MY choice | **we share stories of survival** | *we are beautiful* | we are free | **we are the backbone and muscle of the church** | *our hair* | Black is rebellion | **no one can have your back like another Black woman** | *Black women are gorgeous (incomparably)* | my natural hair is an exquisite crown | **our skin tones are exquisitely beautiful in EVERY shade!** | *we are exquisite from the inside out* | my extra bit of sassiness | **our rhythm** | *locs and natural hair.*

The Beauty of Just Being You

"Dear Beautiful Black Queens…Never underestimate the beauty of just being YOU. Being your authentic self is powerful, sexy, and courageous!"

—**Stephanie Lahart**, author, poet, youth motivational speaker for at-risk teens, and teen mentor

An Exercise in Self-Acceptance

Step One: Identify something that you hate about yourself.

It's hard to have healthy self-esteem when other people put you down. If we have not been taught to love ourselves, then we rely too heavily on what others think and say about us. Many of the people we look to boost our self-esteem don't have the skills to love themselves either, so there is a good chance that we're receiving the wrong message.

Make a list of the role models who have helped shape your self-image: your parents, your brothers and sisters, other relatives, and teachers. What negative messages have you heard about yourself that you remember—comments that you have heard regularly and have taken to heart?

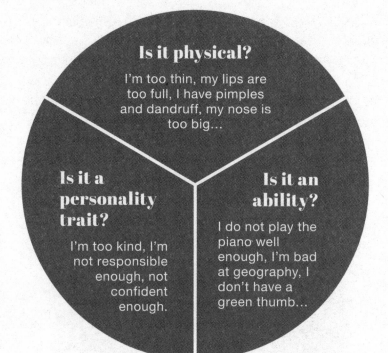

Step Two: Identify what's behind the way you feel about it:

Society's widespread beliefs	"To accept myself as I am right now means I have to give up hope of creating a better version of myself" / "It is pretentious to love myself" / "I cannot be beautiful if I don't have a flat belly"
Conditioning or limiting thoughts	We may have received messages in our childhood or assumed the worst about ourselves from our experiences: "You're all talk and no action" / "You don't know what you want" / "You never get things done."
Comparison	You compare yourself to others and not to your ideal vision of yourself.
Lack of confidence	"I don't deserve to be loved" / "I'm unable to love myself."
Fear	What could happen? What do you fear?
Emotions	Become aware of how you feel. Shame? Failure? A lack of love?

Step Three: Decide whether your flaw is modifiable.

For example, if you have flabby arms, you can decide to lift some weights and change your diet: You have a choice because your arms are simply "in transition."

But if you think you're too short, there's only so much you can do about it except putting on heels, choosing particular outfits, and standing upright. But you might have to learn to love your short, little legs just the way they are.

Step Four: Focus on the positive

Appreciate what you have. Don't obsess about what you don't have. You may have a ginormous belly. But think about how awesome your belly is: it shelters all the organs that allow you to digest your favorite food. By breathing through your belly, you can "massage" your spleen, your liver, and other organs—and this makes you feel good. So, it's a pretty cool belly, thank you very much!

The size of your belly also pushes you to want to exercise—which might never have become your thing otherwise. By running every day, you'll gain confidence, and you'll also be proud of yourself.

You'll gain knowledge of running techniques and nutrition. You'll become more attentive to your body as a whole.

Try to formulate positive sentences: "I'll do better next time" instead of saying: "I'm bad at this." Focus on what you love: "I have a nice mouth" instead of: "My nose is ugly."

What You're Up Against

Black women are three to four times more likely than white women to die from pregnancy-related causes. Research indicates having children can be a life or death choice for Black women. This often happens despite conscious efforts to make the right decisions about health and well-being like doing well in school, saying no to drugs, avoiding teen pregnancy, staying out of debt, and never committing any kind of crime. Infant death rates are also a big problem for Black women, black infants die at 2.2 times the rate of non-Hispanic minorities in the United States.

What are the factors that lead to these problems?

Google it!

AFFIRMATION: Every day is an opportunity for a fresh start. Yesterday is over, and I can't change it now. I'm not afraid of what could go wrong, and I'm excited by what will go right. I know all my problems have solutions, and I'm smart enough to figure them out.

"It's time for you to move, realizing that the thing you are seeking is also seeking you."

—**Iyanla Vanzant**, American inspirational speaker, lawyer, New Thought spiritual teacher, author, life coach, and television personality

"The triumph can't be had without the struggle."

—**Wilma Rudolph**, American sprinter

15 Upbeat Songs for Blue Days

♫ "Celebration," by Kool & The Gang

♫ "Happy," by Pharrell Williams

♫ "What a Wonderful World," by Louis Armstrong

♫ "Don't Worry, Be Happy," by Bobby McFerrin

♫ "Ain't No Mountain High Enough," by Marvin Gaye, Tammi Terrell

♫ "I Can See Clearly Now," by Jimmy Cliff

♫ "Good to Be Alive," by Andy Grammer

♫ "Hakuna Matata," by Nathan Lane, Ernie Sabella, Jason Weaver, and Joseph Williams

♫ "Over the Rainbow," by Israel Kamakawiwo'ole

♫ "Oh, Happiness," by David Crowder Band

♫ "Isn't She Lovely," by Stevie Wonder

♫ "Imagine Me," by Kirk Franklin

♫ "I Can," by Nas

♫ "Keep Ya Head Up," by Tupac

♫ "Happy," by C2C (feat. Derek Martin)

6 (More) Badass Trailblazers in STEM

1940 **Roger Arliner Young** became the first Black American woman to earn a PhD in zoology.

1948 **Dorothy Lavinia Brown** became the first Black American female surgeon in the South.

1950 **Helen Octavia Dickens** became the first Black American female to be admitted to the American College of Surgeons.

1971 **Jane Cooke Wright** became the first Black American woman to become President of the New York Cancer Society.

1981 **Alexa Canady** became the first Black American female to practice neurosurgery.

1993 **Joycelyn Elders,** appointed by President Bill Clinton, became the first Black female to serve as US Surgeon General.

Focus on the Positive

"I don't harp on the negative because if you do, then there's no progression. There's no forward movement. You got to always look on the bright side of things, and we are in control. Like, you have control over the choices you make."

—**Taraji P. Henson**, American actress and author

Changing Your Environment Helps You Remain Positive

Choose the color blue. According to research at the University of Sussex in England, surrounding yourself with the color blue helps calms your mind and improve your mood and ability to concentrate. It increases the speed you can complete a task by up to 25 percent and increases your reaction time by 12 percent. It also improves physical performance. Even if you don't live near the beach, or the sky is filled with clouds today, you can surround yourself with blue, which will increase your self-confidence and reduce your stress.

Listen to upbeat music. If you feel depressed and unmotivated despite the sun shining outside, listening to upbeat music could improve your mood, according to a survey conducted at the University of Missouri. I'm thinking about Pharrell Williams's "Happy." Without a doubt, it soothes my soul when I'm a little sad, tired, or lonely, and I feel in harmony with the world when I listen to it. If you can replace television with music for a while, especially in the morning, that will change everything. Upbeat music will help you concentrate when you need to or let off steam when you're all wound up. It'll relax you when you need it. Listen to upbeat songs that bring pleasant memories, and make you dance or sing.

Stop procrastinating. Do the laundry, take out the trash, and mail that envelope for Christ's sakes! Make a to-do list, and avoid letting tasks accumulate. Otherwise, they'll weight heavily in the back of your mind and spoil all your potential moments of peace and relaxation.

Tidy up. Happiness starts with a pleasant, tidy room. Really. Make your bed; it'll only take a minute, and there's something satisfying and relaxing about it. Also: Don't leave any room empty-handed. Make your trip around the house productive and, when you walk into a room, grab your dirty laundry, put away a dirty mug, and recycle an empty bag. Living in a clean and tidy place brings peace and satisfaction.

Pamper your sense of smell. A pleasant aroma can lift your mood almost immediately (and the opposite is true too). Treat yourself with flowers or scented candles, or get into potpourri making.

Embrace nature. In the United States, a study has shown that walking for one hour among trees can improve memory and attention by 20 percent. In Toronto, researchers have discovered that a fifty-minute daily walk in the wild can treat depression. Outdoor walking strengthens muscles and increases the resistance of the immune system. The breathtaking landscapes, the sounds of nature, being away from the hustle and bustle…all these elements help to stimulate the brain and its creativity. Even if you live in the city, you can still connect with nature: breathe the fresh air; admire the leaves of a nearby tree; try gardening or buy some potted plants; walk barefoot; take a swim in the river or the ocean; sunbathe; hike and/or pick fruit, berries and wildflowers. In a world that goes faster and faster, it is essential to slow down, and you can do that by finding some peace in nature, which has its own slow-jam going on.

Meditate. Regular meditation increases your ability and capacity to feel joy on a daily basis. There is evidence that meditating for a few moments each day helps reduce stress, anxiety, and depression, and therefore makes you happier. By rewiring your brain, meditation allows you to reconnect with yourself, to open yourself to positive things, and to take a step back. You can meditate in the morning to start the day in good mental shape, at lunch to recharge your batteries, or in the evening to get rid of accumulated tension. It's all about finding the right moment. Find a convenient time and an appropriate environment, away from distractions and noise. Plan to wear comfortable and loose clothing.

Meditation on Benevolent Love

There is nothing like a meditation on benevolent love to learn to love oneself. *The steps are as follows:*

Plan for at least fifteen minutes of calm. Sit comfortably with your back straight.

Close your eyes, and start breathing for a few moments. Then, think about someone you love deeply, like a family member or a friend. Feel the love coursing through your veins.

Let this feeling of love grow in you. Then extend it to yourself, and comfort yourself by saying: *I have the right to be loved, I give myself love.*

Minimalize. A recent study shows that the desire for material stuff—regardless of whether we acquire the stuff or not—leads to a drop in happiness by negatively affecting our self-esteem and costing us social relationships. James Roberts, director of the study and marketing professor at Baylor University in Texas, believes that happiness comes from strong relationships with others, and a commitment to our community through volunteer or charitable activities. Different studies confirm that altruism, volunteering, and service—in other words, contributing to the happiness of others—contribute to one's own well-being. Some even conclude that people dedicated to a cause or community organization live longer. Giving money to charities or buying gifts for people you love is good for the soul.

Live in the moment. Most of us have some idea of when or how we will better enjoy life ("When I get this job!" Or "If I get married"), which actually prevents us from being happy, because we're just putting off the joy we could be feeling right now. To think constantly that if we had acted differently in the past, we would be happier today is just as harmful. The past and the future are largely out of our reach. In order to enjoy yourself right now, stop paying too much attention to what *was* and what *could be*, and learn to take advantage of what's all around you this minute.

Just like the past, the future may be a trap—a source of worry and fear. But sometimes, when things are depressing, a goal can help you move forward: "Okay, it's not going well for now, but if I can get through this bad moment, I know that I can find happiness afterward."

If you aren't living the life you dream of, identify what you can improve, but don't obsess about it. Some things are impossible to control, and there will always be a new problem or a difficult challenge. The best path forward is to believe that everything gets better. From a neuroscientific point of view, there are a host of studies that show keeping your focus on the present can change brain function in a positive way. The past belongs to the past, and often, it is nostalgia that robs us from our happiness. Yes, yesterday may have been much better than the present, and the future is very scary, but only today matters: the present is all you have, and you will never have anything else. After all, life is a journey, not a destination.

Practice gratitude. Rather than resenting people who have more money or better jobs than you or your family⬛which lowers self-esteem—try appreciating what you do have. Appreciative people are able to feel real joy when other people do well. Take time to congratulate a person for achieving a goal. When you're having a hard day, think of one thing you're proud you achieved, and feel the moment of happiness in your heart. Say "Thank you," because, no matter your accomplishments, somebody helped you. Even when it gets rough, find a way to express your gratitude to others and to yourself.

Forgive. We can be very hard on ourselves, but taking responsibility for our actions doesn't mean punishing ourselves. Forgive yourself. People who love themselves learn from their mistakes, accept that everyone makes them, and forgive themselves. It is important that you forgive yourself so that you can move forward. How? Remind yourself that you acted in the best possible way in light of the knowledge and level of wisdom you had at the time. Treat yourself kindly—with respect, patience, and gentleness. Also, stop blaming others for what you do not have or how you feel or don't feel. Stop giving up your power and, instead, take responsibility for your life.

Stop complaining. Stop feeling sorry for yourself and thinking about the ways you've failed. Believe in yourself, and don't believe everything your mind says to you, especially if those thoughts are negative or wear you out. Stop complaining about situations, things, and people you can't change. Nobody or nothing can make you unhappy unless you allow it. It's not the situation that triggers these feelings in you but how you see it. Also, avoid spending too much time with people who are constantly negative. There are many people like this, and even if you like these people, interacting with them may hurt you in the long run. Attitude is as contagious as the flu, so keep yourself protected from bad vibes. Be aware that they are negative, and see them from time to time because you enjoy them, but don't let them rub off on you.

Accept change. Change is the only thing that will allow you to improve your life and the lives of those around you. Do not resist it.

What You're Up Against

Are there any Black women currently running America's biggest corporations? In the history of the United States, very few Black women have risen to the top positions in major companies. Why do you think there are so few Black American women running Fortune 500 companies in corporate America?

Google It!

AFFIRMATION: I am not my mistakes. I forgive myself for screwing up sometimes. Mistakes help me learn and grow. I get stronger every single day. It's okay not to know everything. There's still so much for me to learn.

"Don't let anyone steal ya joy! There's always someone miserable trying to bring you down...you just wish them well and proceed on enjoying your life."

—**Missy Elliott**, American rapper, singer, songwriter, dancer, and record producer

The Badass Black Girl Playlist

♫ "Independent Woman," by Destiny's Child

♫ "Melanin," by Secrett

♫ "I Am Light," by India.Arie

♫ "Don't Touch My Hair," by Solange

♫ "R. E. S. P. E. C. T.," by Aretha Franklin

♫ "You Gotta Be," by Des'ree

♫ "Girl on Fire," by Alicia Keys

♫ "Put Your Records On," by Corinne Bailey Rae

♫ "Run the World [Girls]," by Beyoncé

♫ "Control," by Janet Jackson

♫ "I Will Survive," by Gloria Gaynor

♫ "Bossy," by Kelis

♫ "Overcomer," by Mandisa

♫ "Shackles (Praise You)," by Mary Mary

♫ "Wonder Woman," by Lion Babe

♫ "Dance or Die," by Janelle Monáe

♫ "Ooh Child," by The Five Stairsteps

♫ "Black Truck," by Mereba

♫ "Kolobi," by Tiwa Savage

♫ "Black Woman," by Danielle Brooks

♫ "Young, Gifted and Black," by Aretha Franklin

♫ "Encourage Yourself," by Donald Lawrence & The Tri-City Singers

♫ "Grown Woman," by Beyoncé

♫ "Pieces of Me," by Ledisi

♫ "Blk Girl Soldier," by Jamila Woods

♫ "Due West," by Kelsey Lu

♫ "Way Back," by Amber Mark

♫ "Black Girl Magik," by Sampa the Great feat. Nicole Gumbe

♫ "I Owe You Nothing," by Seinabo Sey

♫ "I am not my hair," by India.Arie feat. Akon

♫ "New Agenda," by Janet Jackson

♪ "Freedom," by Beyoncé

♪ "Ladies First," by Queen Latifah feat. Monie Love

♪ "Feeling Good," by Nina Simone

♪ "Q. U. E. E. N.," by Janelle Monáe

♪ "Unpretty," by TLC

♪ "Black Girl Pain," by Talib Kweli

♪ "I'm Coming Out," by Diana Ross

♪ "Womanifesto," by Jill Scott

♪ "Hero," by Mariah Carey

♪ "Good Woman Down," by Mary J. Blige

♪ "Superwoman," by Alicia Keys

♪ "Kelly," by Kelly Rowland

♪ "Video [Because I'm a Queen]," by India.Arie

♪ "River," by Ibeyi

♪ "Masterpiece," by Jasmine Sullivan

♪ "Pretty Girl Rock," by Keri Hilson

♪ "Bag Lady," by Erykah Badu

♪ "Do My Thing," by Estelle

♪ "Proud," by Heather Small

♪ "Closer," by Goapele

♫ "A Beautiful Day," by India.Arie

♫ "Higher Than This," by Ledisi

♫ "No Regrets," by Elisabeth Withers

♫ "Strength, Courage and Wisdom," by India.Arie

♫ "Black Gold," by Esperanza Spalding (feat. Algebra Blessett)

♫ "Star People," by Fertile Ground

♫ "Brown Skin Girls," by Beyoncé

"Greatness is not measured by what a man or woman accomplishes, but by the opposition he or she has overcome to reach his goals."

—**Dorothy Height**, revolutionary leader of the civil rights movement

6 (More) Badass Trailblazers in Politics and Law (2010–NOW)

Rep. Ilhan Omar (D-MN) smiles to the crowd during her address at the 2019 Youth Climate Strike in Washington D.C.

2015 **Loretta Lynch** was the first Black woman to become US Attorney General.

2015 **Paulette Brown** became the first Black American woman President at the American Bar Association.

2016 **Carla Hayden** became the first woman and first Black American to be the Librarian of Congress.

2017 **Andrea Jenkins** became the first openly transgender person of color elected to public office in the United States.

2018 **Stacey Abrams** of Georgia became the first Black American woman to be a major party nominee for state governor.

2019 **Ilhan Omar** became the first Somali-American Muslim person to become a legislator when she is elected to Congress representing Minnesota.

Think About It

"I have found that among its other benefits, giving liberates the soul of the giver."

—**Maya Angelou**, American poet, writer, singer, memoirist, and civil rights activist

What does the word "beauty" mean to you? | What do you think makes a person attractive? | **Can you name someone you think is attractive and say why?** | *What's the best compliment you've ever received?* | Do you like it when people tell you you are beautiful? | **Do you like the way you look?** | *What do you think it means when people say that beauty comes from the inside?* | Do you think Barbie dolls, Disney princesses, and superheroes give little boys and girls unrealistic body expectations? | **Do you prefer it when your mom wears makeup?** | *How old do you think a girl should be before she's allowed to wear makeup?*

| What is most important to girls today in terms of their self-identity? | **What influences how girls act, look, and think about themselves and others?** | *What roles do movies, television, music, magazines, peers, beauty and clothing industries, and parents play in influencing a girl's identity and well-being?* | What is the modern feminine ideal? | **What influences are informing your responses?** | *How would your parents answer these same questions?* | Statistics tell us most adolescent American girls are unhappy with the way they look. Does this echo your own and your friends' attitudes? | **How are female bodies represented in advertisements, television, movies, and print media?** | *How do these representations influence the way girls feel about their bodies and the way they dress?* | What do the manufacturers of body products and projects such as makeup, clothing, diet aids, and plastic surgery stand to gain from making girls unhappy about their bodies? | **What television programs, movies, music videos, and advertisements do these photographs remind you of? Explain.** | *Name several female media idols who are role models for girls today.* | How does the sexualization of contemporary media idols influence the way girls look and act? | **How powerful is peer pressure in influencing the body and clothing standards girls feel they should attain?** | *How does peer pressure support girls who maintain these standards while rejecting those who do not?* | How powerful is parental involvement in influencing the body ideals and standards of girls? | **Does parental involvement sometimes perpetuate cultural standards of image?** | *Is parental involvement powerful enough to help girls overcome the stigma that can accompany not fitting into peers' image standards?*

Do Not Underestimate Your Ability to Bounce Back

"Just remember the world is not a playground but a schoolroom. Life is not a holiday but an education. One eternal lesson for us all: to teach us how better we should love."

—**Barbara Jordan**, American lawyer, educator, politician, and leader of the civil rights movement

Dear Badass Black Girls,

When we learn to let go, we find a way to happiness even when it's different from what we planned. We also bounce back from bad experiences much faster than we expect.

Letting go is NOT about rejecting, ignoring, or avoiding our pain. It's much healthier to welcome emotions, positive and negative, and not fight against them, so that you can then more easily accept them. Letting go is knowing how to take a step back to free yourself from your emotions and fears.

According to American-born Swiss singer, songwriter, and actress Tina Turner, "Sometimes, you've got to let everything go—purge yourself. If you are unhappy with anything…whatever is bringing you down, get rid of it. Because you'll find that when you're free, your true creativity, your true self comes out." Letting go allows us to find inner peace instead of fighting against ourselves. It's a state of balance between who we are, what we want, and what goes on inside of us.

No more dark thoughts. Do not torture your mind with things that are not worth your time. By remaining optimistic and practicing gratitude, you can more easily find solutions to your problems. Be realistic, but remain positive.

Kenbe,
MJ

What You're Up Against

The United States has a huge prison population, and it's growing rapidly. Black Americans make up a stunning majority of US prisoners compared to the population outside correctional facilities:

- Black women are more than twice as likely to receive a prison sentence as white women for committing the same crime, and when they are sentenced for committing a crime, they are more likely to receive a longer sentence. This also holds true for Black girls in the juvenile justice system.

- If Black people went to prison at the same rate as white people, the prison population in the United States would decrease by about 40 percent!

- One out of every nine Black American children has a parent who is in prison right now or who served time in the past.

What's going on?

Adultification bias in schools (see page 82) is a major part of the problem. Black girls are often punished harshly with zero-tolerance policies that subject them to violence, arrest, suspension and/or expulsion with no chance of reformation, even for minor mistakes. These policies create something called the "School-to-Prison" pipeline.

"School-to-Prison" Pipeline: A Few Examples

2014 After she wrote "Hi" on the wall of her middle school's locker room, a twelve-year-old Black female student from Georgia faced criminal charges and expulsion. That same year, a Detroit honors student and high school senior was suspended for the entire school year for accidentally bringing a pocket-knife to a school football game.

2013 An eight-year-old Black girl in Illinois was arrested for having a meltdown and throwing a temper tantrum.

2013 A sixteen-year-old Black girl in Alabama was hit with a book by a teacher for falling asleep in class. The student suffered from several medical conditions that increase sleepiness including diabetes, asthma, and sleep apnea. That same student was later arrested and had to be hospitalized because of the severity of the injuries she received during her arrest.

2013 A sixteen-year-old Black girl in Florida caused a minor explosion during a science experiment on school grounds and was arrested. That same year, a twelve-year-old Black girl in an Orlando public school was ordered to change the look of her natural hair or face expulsion from the school.

2007 A six-year-old Black female student in Florida threw a tantrum in her classroom and was arrested. That same year, in a California school, A sixteen-year-old black female student was arrested when she didn't pick up her dropped cake to a school officer's satisfaction.

(Source: The Black Girls Matter Report, published by the Center for Intersectionality and Social Policy Studies and the African American Policy Forum)

Black girls go to prison more than any other group of girls in the United States. They face a greater likelihood of being killed in an act of violence and are much more likely to be unemployed, even without a criminal record. What factors cause this problem? What kinds of crimes put most Black girls and women in our prisons? Who in society benefits from keeping Black people jailed?

Google it!

"I am a woman who came from the cotton fields of the South. From there I was promoted to the washtub. From there I was promoted to the cook kitchen. And from there I promoted myself into the business of manufacturing hair goods and preparations… I have built my own factory on my own ground."

—**Madam C. J. Walker**, American entrepreneur, philanthropist, and a political and social activist.

3 Badass Trailblazers in Business

Ursula Burns, Chairman and CEO, Xerox, speaks during the 2012 Most Powerful Women Summit.

1903 **Maggie Lena Walker** became the first Black American woman to establish and serve as President of a US bank when she took over St. Luke Penny Savings Bank (since 1930 the Consolidated Bank and Trust Company) in Richmond, Virginia.

1910 **Madam C.J. Walker** was the first Black American female millionaire. She made her fortune in haircare.

2009 **Ursula Burns** of Xerox Corporation became the first Black American female CEO of a Fortune 500 company.

Other powerful Black women in business:

Several women of color were named on America's Richest Self-Made Women list published by *Forbes* in 2019:

- Beyoncé

- Janice Bryant Howroyd

- Sheila Johnson

- Rihanna

- Oprah

- Serena Williams

Why were these women on the list?

Google It!

How to Bounce Back

*"You wanna fly? You got to give up
the sh*t that weighs you down."*

—**Toni Morrison**, an American novelist, essayist, editor,
teacher, and professor emeritus at Princeton University

Dear Badass Black Girl,

Concentrate on the positive.

Be proud. Be fierce.

Learn to love the girl you are, because you deserve to be loved exactly as you are right now. But don't be afraid to become the person you dream of becoming.

Trust yourself. Make mistakes.

Don't forget to breathe.

Show empathy.

Open your heart, your arms, your eyes, and your mind.

Look around you.

Listen to others.

Take notes.

Kenbe,
MJ

Turn Your Setbacks into Success

"Sometimes it's worse to win a fight than to lose."

—**Billie Holiday**, American jazz singer

Dear Badass Black Girl,

After a failure, it is not always easy to get up. Here are some tips to turn your setbacks into a step toward success.

Take it easy. Take a step back, and focus for a while on your hobbies or volunteer activities—whatever will nurse your confidence back to health and keep you from developing negative beliefs about yourself and your abilities.

Accept your new reality. There is no denying it: failure is hard to accept on an emotional level. Anger and denial quickly follow the initial shock. You might say, "I don't care," "They were idiots, anyway," or "I quit" because you haven't accepted your new situation. This is perfectly normal, but you have to overcome this stage and accept your new reality. Learn to tell the difference between facts, opinions, and feelings. Recognize your emotions. Accept your defeat without dramatizing it.

Assess. Examine the thing you absolutely wanted but did not get (For example, "I wanted to make the cheerleading squad" or "I wanted to make the soccer team"). What exactly went south? Put aside your emotions (for just a few moments), and try to understand how you got to where you are. "If I had to do it again, what would I do differently?" Leave your usual environment, and go somewhere where you can view the situation from a different angle. Then, you can start to figure out what exactly prevented this dream from coming true: what people and/or events influenced you, and what minor or major missteps did you make?

You have to consider the weight of your failure in the grand scheme of things and put everything in perspective. Will it matter in five years? In twenty years? From there, it's about getting back into your groove, building a new action plan, and moving on. Once this painful task has been done—a job that many people avoid doing—you will be better prepared to imagine a "redefined self." In other words, you can start working now on the person you want to become, instead of comparing yourself to others or trying to catch up with the person you wanted to be before.

Establish a new action plan. Take a good look at yourself and the circumstances. What does this situation teach you about yourself, about your relationship with others, about your limits and basic needs? Make a list of your resources—your qualities and skills. Exercise and/or meditation can help you see things more clearly and refocus. How can you make up for the shortcomings you discovered? For example, if you've learned you lose your temper when under stress, you may decide to commit to regular breathing exercises to control your level of anxiety. Plan for a new future with new projects and goals that will motivate you and restore your self-confidence.

Clean up your address book, and create distance from people who make you feel guilty or tend to bring up your shortcomings (and theirs) over and over and over again. You don't need to absorb the stress of others in addition to your own. Only maintain relationships that bring comfort. If your family brings you stress at home, spend more time with friends, or find a quiet place of your own where you can start to move past this.

Move forward. If you catch yourself thinking you'll repeat the failure, STOP. Tell yourself that every situation is different. The next time you have to prove yourself during an interview, an exam, or a competition, the conditions, the subjects, and the other people involved will have changed. And, *you* will have changed. Set realistic, reasonable goals you can place on a realistic timeline. Then, stick to the plan!

Choose new skills. A wonderful way to increase self-esteem is by developing new skills. Have you always dreamed of climbing, painting or joining a dance troupe? Sign up now or start with a YouTube lesson! Doing a new activity that you love will allow you to discover skills you haven't tried until now.

Focus on what's going well. The brain is programmed to spot negative events in advance to avoid dangers. But what was useful back in our cavewoman days is no longer necessary today. According to neuropsychologist Rick Hanson, it's important to be aware every day of things that make you feel good.

Each day, make a list of three moments during the day that brought you a sense of well-being or satisfaction. This can be something very simple: the aroma of coffee or listening to a Diana Ross album. Happiness is sometimes in the small things. Writing them down daily can help increase our ability to be happy.

Kenbe,
MJ

What Are You Up Against?

The Jezebel/Video Vixen represents a sexualized Black woman. The term Jezebel comes from the Biblical Queen who turned her husband against God. Since slavery, Black women have been sexualized in demeaning ways that focus on sexuality and appearance but make no room for our brainpower. These images are all over the media. You can see them often represented in rap and hip-hop videos. Black women, particularly professional Black women, work hard to dispel the Jezebel/Video Vixen image.

What ways can Black women work to ensure they are seen for more than their bodies and sex appeal?

Google it!

Think About It: Are You Too Woke?

"Someone was hurt before you, wronged before you, hungry before you, frightened before you, beaten before you, humiliated before you, raped before you…yet, someone survived… You can do anything you choose to do."

—**Maya Angelou**, American poet, singer, memoirist, and civil rights activist

If you haven't heard this term yet, you will eventually: *Microaggression.* Unfortunately, it's something all Black girls deal with at some point or another. The term was first coined in the 1970s by a psychiatrist named Chester Pierce. A microaggression is an indignity that individuals in minority groups are subjected to, either intentionally or subconsciously due to racism. These aren't the blatant hostilities, but they can sting when you encounter them, and often, it's a struggle to figure out how you'll handle them when they pop up. A couple examples include: Being told, "you're pretty…for a Black girl" (or replace "pretty" with "smart," "pretty," "well-spoken," etc.). Or even having someone tell you, "When I look at you, I don't see your color." (Makes you want to suggest they schedule an eye exam, huh?)

In her column, "On the Run from Mediocrity," Victoria Prester writes about being worried that "all of this wokeness can lead to an over-analysis of social situations." Some examples of when she was subjected to other people's subconscious racism and microaggression include: a waitress forgetting only her order out of a large dining party; welcoming visitors to her home for the first time and hearing them remark that they were surprised her family could live in "such a nice house."

She argues that for her, the healthiest choice she can make sometimes is to...let it go. She doesn't speak up *every single time* she faces racial bias or a microaggression, because she might forget to live a life filled with joy, and it wears a person out to fight ignorance all the time. She writes, "I must choose the battles I want to fight against discrimination, because trying to fight or even mentally analyze all of them takes too much mental energy, can take away too much peace of mind."

What's your take? Is it your responsibility to take a stand every single time? If not, when do you let it go?

Practice Gratitude

"Be thankful for what you have; you'll end up having more. If you concentrate on what you don't have, you will never, ever have enough."

—**Oprah Winfrey**, American media executive, actress, talk show host, television producer, and philanthropist.

Dear Badass Black Girl,

It pays to practice gratitude. When you practice being thankful for what you have and those who helped you along the way, you become more upbeat, more confident, more efficient, less stressed, less jealous of other people, and more satisfied with your life.

Here are ten exercises to bring gratitude into your life:

Three good things: This is one of the easiest and best-known exercises to practice gratitude. Every night before going to bed, take a few minutes to think back to the day that has just passed. Focus on positive events, and find three things you can be thankful for. This exercise will be particularly useful after a tough day because it will help you remember the positive parts of your day even if the whole day felt like a nightmare or you think you made one mistake after another. Maybe, even though you woke up a half-hour late and had to skip breakfast, you still made it to the bus stop in time to catch your ride to school. Maybe you sprained your ankle in gym class, but you were helped to the nurse's office by classmates who showed you how much they care about you. There's usually something positive to be found in any situation. It might take some digging to find it, but you can do it!

You will find you can still find positives: a pleasant discussion with a classmate, a free spot in a crowded parking lot, your baby sister who ran into arms when she returned from kindergarten, a delicious meal, a postcard from the other side of the world... There are always reasons to feel happy.

Remember to thank life for these little gifts, these little pleasures. You can also do this exercise when you wake up or at breakfast time, but what a happy way to fall asleep, with your heart filled with joy and gratitude…

The gratitude journal or gratitude book: Take a notebook and a pen and, as for the first exercise, think back over your day. This time, note three to five things you can give thanks for once a day, once or more a week. Find a comfortable pace so this is an on-going commitment. Completing your gratitude journal should be a pleasure, not a chore. Put it on your nightstand, and fill it when you feel like it.

If you prefer new technologies, another variation of the gratitude journal is to take pictures of things you feel grateful for. You can try the experience over a week by taking a picture a day, for example. You can also test apps like *Gratitude Journal 365* or *HappyFeed— Gratitude Journal.* Another possibility: make these images into a beautiful collage you can hang on your wall to keep the things you are thankful for on your mind.

The letter of gratitude: This is a powerful exercise in giving thanks and showing appreciation to others. Write a letter to someone who matters tremendously to you—someone who has inspired you or currently inspires you to be as badass as you are, but you have not yet taken the time or the trouble to thank. It can be a teacher, a mentor, a parent, a grandparent, a friend, a coworker, or anyone else. Someone who has helped you, who inspires you, who has shown kindness or generosity, or someone you can rely on, that you are genuinely grateful to have in your life. In short, someone to whom you genuinely appreciate and gratitude.

You don't need to write a novel (unless you want to one day), but be specific about what that person has done for you and how they made your life better. If they've been a role model, point out the qualities you appreciate in them. Explain to them what fills you with gratitude. You can choose a handwritten version that's more personal, and you can mail the letter, hand-deliver it, or email it. However you go about doing it, it's important to let people who lift you up know that you appreciate the difference they've made in your life.

The gratitude visit: If you aren't shy about showing your feelings, one step above the letter of gratitude is the visit of gratitude. Instead of sending your letter, you make an appointment with the rock stars in your life and read it in person. Tell them you want to meet to discuss something, but don't mention the letter of gratitude. Stay vague. Keep this a surprise.

When you are in front of the person, tell them that you want to read a letter describing how thankful you are to them. Ask them not to interrupt you until you have finished reading your letter. Take your time. As you read, try to pay attention to the reactions of the recipient, but also pay attention to yours.

At the end of the reading, discuss your feelings—this exercise often brings up strong emotions. If you live far away from this person, new technologies can make it easier. You can have a video chat over Skype, Google Hangouts or social networks.

The jar of gratitude: To create your jar of gratitude, you will need paper, a pen, a jar, and whatever decorations you think will reflect your personality: stickers, paint, glitter, ribbons, glue, etc. Then, decorate it. Make this a jar that fills your heart with joy when you look at it. Once your jar is ready, place it in a room where you are sure to see it every day. Ideally, choose a place where you spend the end of the day: if you put it in the bathroom, you will see it when you brush your teeth or, if you place it on your bedside table, you can look at it before going to bed.

Then, as you did in the exercise above, practice thinking about three events of your day for which you feel grateful. It can be small pleasures like tasting your favorite pastry, receiving a call from your best friend, or enjoying a beautiful sunset… Every day, note these moments of happiness on slips of paper and place them in your jar of gratitude. As your jar fills up, you will realize that you have plenty of reasons to be grateful. If you ever feel a little down, open your jar and pull out some memories to remind yourself it ain't all that bad.

Some people prefer to put a coin in their jar of gratitude whenever they feel grateful. Then, once filled, you can donate it to a cause you want to help out.

The gratitude box: As with the jar of gratitude, get a box and anything you think is necessary to make it pretty. This time, the exercise involves writing messages of gratitude to the person of your choice. If you're out of inspiration for ways people have helped you out, you can thank people for some of the special qualities that make them unique, write down things you like about this person, what they taught you, how they inspire you, and just say thanks for being part of your life.

Here are some examples:

> Thank you for your patience at the doctor's office | Your kindness touches me so much | Thank you for your kindness to me | Thank you for being here for me, I'm so lucky to have a friend like you | What I like about you is that you always believe in me | Thank you for supporting me and encouraging me with all my projects | I like to talk about how life is going with you. It makes me feel like I can do better | Thank you for being yourself | I love you as you are

Open your heart, and let your feelings speak! Fill your box of gratitude with all your little words, and offer it up on a special occasion. I think it's a wonderful gift idea for Valentine's Day, a loved one's birthday, a teacher, Father's Day or Mother's Day or even Christmas.

The gratitude walk: This exercise of gratitude couldn't be simpler. It combines the benefits of physical activity, gratitude, and mindfulness meditation. Go for a walk somewhere where you are close to nature if possible. Walk slowly, and focus on the present moment. Pay attention to all the wonders that surround you, everything that can give you pleasure, and what you are grateful for in this moment. It may be, for example, the song of birds, the beauty of butterflies, the color of trees, the smell of flowers, the wind in your hair, the heat of the sun on your skin… Let yourself be overwhelmed by this deep sense of well-being and gratitude. Allow yourself at least twenty to thirty minutes of walking. This is the time your body needs to secrete feel-good endorphins. The practice of regular physical activity has a positive impact on your morale, your level of stress and the quality of your sleep. In addition to allowing you to express your gratitude, this exercise is perfect for clearing your head of your worries and anxieties.

Gratitude Meditation: Here's another exercise that combines meditation and gratitude, two activities that help elevate your level of happiness. To practice a gratitude meditation, sit comfortably in a place where you know you won't be disturbed. Close your eyes, and focus on your breathing. Let all your cares out as you exhale stress and drama, and breathe in peace. Breathe deeply until you reach a state of calm. Pay attention to things around you that you can hear or feel: The breeze on your skin, the birds in the trees, the traffic in the distance, the rush of water, whatever is in the place you are at—and say inwardly, "For all this, I am grateful."

Next, think about the important people in your life: your family members, your friends, your boyfriend/girlfriend… Soak up the love and gratitude you feel for them, and in the same way, say, "thank you," inwardly, "For all these people, I am grateful." Mentally review the things that make you grateful for life, not forgetting what we tend to take for granted, such as the chance to be alive and healthy, our ability to see, hear, walk, and communicate, You can also visualize the physical things you have—such as technology—and how they make your life easier. Take the necessary time: two, five, ten, or even fifteen minutes, and give thanks.

The gratitude inventory: List a hundred things that you are grateful for. Yes, one hundred things. I know, at first, it may seem impossible to find that many, but they are there. If it helps, create categories: your possessions, your relationship, the activities you enjoy, your current job or your previous jobs, your qualities and traits, outings, concerts, trips you've made, and all the places you've visited, your health, and that of your loved ones, all your life experiences you are proud of, awards that you have obtained, sports or academic achievements, or clubs you belong to. Think about your interests. For example, if you're interested in entertainment, you could think about someone you met who you admire, like a recording artist or an actress you're a big fan of. Maybe you went to a concert where the tickets sold out quickly. Maybe you've won a contest or prize money. Once you get started, you'll find that you will fill your gratitude inventory with a lot more ease than you thought.

The gratitude stone: We get so wrapped up in the routine of everyday life that it's not always easy to think of practicing gratitude spontaneously, let alone regularly. Here is a little exercise that can help you… Choose a rock or a small stone that you like, regardless of its appearance. The stone here is nothing but a symbol, a physical object whose purpose is to remind you to practice gratitude. You can just as easily replace it with any other small object that means "gratitude" to you. Put your stone of gratitude in your pocket, in your purse, or leave it out on your desk. Choose a place where you are sure you can see it all day long, whenever you want to. Whenever you see it or touch it, if it's in your pocket, take a break and think of at least one thing for which you feel gratitude or joy right then, at that very moment. Another technique is to program one or more alarms on your phone. For example, one when you get up in the morning and one in the evening at bedtime. If you use this method, remember the positive events that occurred between the two alarms. Feel and express your gratitude.

*"Life is short, and it's up to
you to make it sweet."*

—**Sadie Delany**, American educator and civil rights pioneer

30 Days of Gratitude

Day 1:

What does gratitude mean to you?

Day 2:

What does "the grass is always greener on the other side" mean to you? What are you taking for granted that you should be thankful for?

Day 3:

Write about a happy memory.

Day 4:

Write about a place you've been to that you're grateful for.

Day 5:

What's something you're grateful to have today that you didn't have a year ago? Write a letter or note to your older self, and list five things you'll be grateful for when you reach her age.

Day 6:

What's a simple pleasure that you're grateful for?

Day 7:

What's something about your body or health that you're grateful for?

Day 8:

Look around the room, and write about everything you see that you're grateful for. Then, open the door or window and look outside. What's something you're grateful for outside? What are you thankful for in nature?

Day 9:

What's an accomplishment you're proud of? What skill(s) do you have that you're grateful for?

Day 10:

What mistake or failure are you grateful for?

Day 11:

What's a possession that makes your life easier?

Day 12:

Open your phone or photo album, and find a photo that you like. Why are you grateful for this photo?

Day 13:

What have you been given that you're grateful for?

Day 14:

What public service or organization are you grateful for (i.e. the library or fire department)?

Day 15:

What book(s) are you grateful for?

Day 16:

What piece of clothing or furniture are you grateful for?

Day 17:

List three things that made you smile today.

Day 18:

Recall a time you needed and received encouragement.

Day 19:

What is a luxury you are thankful for?

Day 20:

What's a tradition you're grateful for?

Day 21:

What's one of your personality traits that you're grateful for?

Day 22:

What's something you made recently that you're grateful for?

Day 23:

What will show your family you are grateful for them today?

Day 24:

Why are you grateful for your country?

Day 25:

What are the lyrics from a song that inspires you?

Day 26:

What's something that you bought recently that you're grateful for?

Day 27:

What is the most unexpected compliment you ever got?

Day 28:

What time of day are you grateful for?

Day 29:

What is one scent you're grateful for?

Day 30:

Who are you grateful for? It could be a friend, a teacher or mentor, a family member, or anyone else in your life who makes you feel safe. It could even be an artist, an author, or a musician.

"You are the designer of your destiny; you are the author of your story."

—**Lisa Nichols**, life coach and motivational speaker

Life Is Pretty Badass

Dear Badass Black Girl,

You have all the keys you need to work your Black girl magic! Once you start practicing, you'll better understand how these little positive habits can bring feelings of well-being to you as well as those you express your gratitude to.

The exercises in this book are all ways to gently reprogram your brain to focus on the positive. You don't have to practice them all, but do try them out to find the ones that work for you. You'll know which ones are effective, because they'll bring you the most happiness and satisfaction.

Choose to do these on a schedule that suits you, but remember, regular practice and training will help you see results much faster than randomly reaching for one when you're desperate for a boost. Of course, this is also the field guide to reach for in times of desperation, but make it part of your routine to reap the biggest benefits.

You live in a remarkable time when the world is changing rapidly, and you can be as big a part of those changes as you allow yourself to imagine. Life is pretty badass, isn't it? Be grateful you are living it!

Kenbe,
MJ

About the Author

Born in Port-au-Prince, Haiti, MJ Fievre currently writes from Miami.

MJ's publishing career began as a teenager in Haiti. Her first mystery novel, *Le Feu de la Vengeance*, was published at the age of sixteen. At nineteen, she signed her first book contract with Hachette-Deschamps, in Haiti, for the publication of a young adult book titled *La Statuette Maléfique*. As of today, MJ has authored nine books in French that are widely read in Europe and the French Antilles.

In the United States, One Moore Book released MJ's first children's book, *I Am Riding*, which is part of OMB's Haiti series edited by Edwidge Danticat. Beating Windward Press published MJ's memoir, *A Sky the Color of Chaos*, about her childhood in Haiti during the brutal regime of Jean-Bertrand Aristide. MJ's short stories and poems in English have appeared in various anthologies, including *Flashes of Horror* (Horror Without Borders, 2019) and *Making Good Time* (Jai Alai Books, 2019), and her plays have been performed at the Miami MicroTheater and at the O, Miami Festival's Poetry Press Week.

MJ earned a bachelor's degree in Education from Barry University and an MFA from the creative writing program at Florida International University. She taught writing for eight years at Nova Middle School in Davie and later became a writing professor at Broward College and Miami Dade College.

Mango Publishing, established in 2014, publishes an eclectic list of books by diverse authors—both new and established voices—on topics ranging from business, personal growth, women's empowerment, LGBTQ studies, health, and spirituality to history, popular culture, time management, decluttering, lifestyle, mental wellness, aging, and sustainable living. We were recently named 2019's #1 fastest growing independent publisher by *Publishers Weekly*. Our success is driven by our main goal, which is to publish high quality books that will entertain readers as well as make a positive difference in their lives.

Our readers are our most important resource; we value your input, suggestions, and ideas. We'd love to hear from you—after all, we are publishing books for you!

Please stay in touch with us and follow us at:

Facebook: Mango Publishing
Twitter: @MangoPublishing
Instagram: @MangoPublishing
LinkedIn: Mango Publishing
Pinterest: Mango Publishing

Sign up for our newsletter at www.mangopublishinggroup.com and receive a free book!

Join us on Mango's journey to reinvent publishing, one book at a time.